METHODS
OF
TEACHING
ENGLISH

Dr. Muhammad Ali Alkhuli

Publisher: DAR ALFALAH	الناشر: دار الفلاح للنشر والتوزيع
P.O.Box 818	ص.ب 818
Swaileh11910	صويلح 11910
Jordan	الأردن
Tel & Fax 009626-5411547	هاتف وفاكس 009626-5411547
E-mail: books@daralfalah.com	
Website: www.daralfalah.com	

1

2006 Edition

Publisher: DAR ALFALAH	الناشر: دار الفلاح للنشر والتوزيع
P.O.Box 818	ص.ب 818
Swaileh 11910	صويلح 11910
Jordan	الأردن
Tel & Fax 009626-5411547	هاتف وفاكس 009626-5411547

E-mail: books@daralfalah.com
Website: www.daralfalah.com

رقم الإيداع لدى دائرة المكتبة الوطنية
2033/11/1999

Class No.   420.7

Author: Muhammad Ali Alkhuli

Title: Methods of Teaching English

Subject Heading: 1. English Language
                 2.Teaching

Notes:
           Prepared by National Library, Jordan

رقم الإجازة المتسلسل لدى دائرة المطبوعات والنشر (الأردن)   ١٥١٥ /١١/ ١٩٩٩

ISBN   9 9 5 7-- 4 0 1-- 1 3 -- 9   (ك

PREFACE

    This book is written with the purpose of helping university students majoring in English and who are planning to teach English as a foreign language after their graduation. It can also be beneficial to English teachers in service. Further, a great deal of material included in this book applies to teaching any foreign language.

    The book starts with a general introduction to language, linguistics, teaching approaches, and other topics of an introductory nature. Then it devotes separate chapters to deal with the methods of teaching pronuncia-
tion, grammar, vocabulary, reading, and writing of the foreign language in general and English in particular. Moreover, the book deals with how to test each language skill and how to make use of audio-visuals aids.

    It has been made clear on many occasions in this book that the ideas given are not inevitable imperatives, but they are merely suggestions. In other words, teachers are encouraged to feel free to try other methods if they wish since it is not among our goals to chain student teachers or regular teachers, but to offer them a variety of methods which may be helpful.

    In addition, each chapter is followed by some questions or exercises, the purposes of which are to stimulate students to think creatively, read critically, and evaluate objectively. Students are advised to do those exercises and give them the attention they require.

    Finally, I would like to thank Dr. Tawfeek Yousef and Mr. Bruce E. Mellon for their valuable comments.

Dr. Muhammad Ali Alkhuli

CONTENTS

INTRODUCTION

In this introductory chapter, there will be a brief discussion of language in general concerning its nature and definition. Further, this chapter
will introduce the different branches of linguistics because related terms
will be frequently used in this book.

In addition, the chapter will explain the importance of English in the Arab world and the
different approaches and theories used in teaching foreign languages. It will also deal with
other topics related to the field of foreign language teaching such as program types and
influential variables.

I. 1. Language:

There are several possible definitions of language, but there is one particular definition that
may be most related to our purposes here. Accord-ing to this definition, language is an
arbitrary system of vocal symbols used to communicate ideas and express feelings among the
members of a cer-
tain social community.

This definition emphasizes several points:

1. Language is a system. This indicates that language is systematic at phonetic, phonemic,
morphemic, morphological, syntactic, and semantic levels.

2. The system of language is arbitrary. This arbitrariness means that
there is no logical reason why a certain language behaves as it does. For
example, there is no reason why the subject or the doer in an English state-

ment comes before the verb whereas in Arabic the verb may come before the doer.

3. Language is basically vocal, which implies that language is mainly an oral activity and that writing is merely a secondary form of language. In other words, language is speech and writing is a representation of speech.

4. Language is symbols of referents, which implies that words, for example, are not identical with what they refer to, but just symbols for them.

5. The function of language is not only to convey ideas, but also feelings. In addition, one has to get acquainted with other important features of language such as:

1. Language is diversified into social dialects, which are linguistic varieties that mark social classes that usually correspond to economic and educational levels.

2. Language is also diversified into geographical dialects which mark linguistic differences among the districts of a certain country.

3. Language usually has formal and informal varieties, i.e., standard and colloquial dialects.

4. Language is expressed in different media : the oral medium and the graphic medium.

5. Each individual speaks language in a rather unique manner called an idiolect.

6. Each language has these sequential levels of structure : phonemic, morphemic, lexical, and syntactic levels. These levels are hierarchically inter-related : phonemes string together to build morphemes, which may combine together to form lexemes, which are in turn juxtaposed to form sentences.

1. 2. Linguistics:

Linguistics is the science that with language. This science branches into many fields:

1. Phonetics. Phonetics is a science that deals with the production, transmission, and perception of the phones of language, i.e., its sounds.

2. Articulatory phonetics. It deals with the articulation of speech sounds.

3. Acoustic phonetics. It deals with the transmission of speech sounds.

4. Auditory phonetics. It deals with the perception of speech sounds.

5. Phonemics. It is a science that classifies phones into phonemes. In other words, it groups phones into allophones belonging to certain phonemes. Thus it is a science that deals with the procedure of phoneme discovery.

6. Morphology. It is a science that deals with morphemes, the smallest meaningful units in language.

7. Syntax. It deals with the order of words within larger units such as phrases, clauses, and sentences.

8.   Grammar. It is morphology and syntax.

9.   Semantics. It is the science of meaning.

10.   Descriptive linguistics. It describes the phonological and grammatical aspects of language as it is, not as it should be.

11.   Comparative linguistics. It compares languages of common origin.

12.   Historical linguistics. It traces changes undergone by a certain language through centuries.

13. Applied linguistics. It is a science that deals with the application of significant linguistic findings in the field of teaching language to native speakers or foreigners.

1. 3. Why English ?

In the previous section, we have got acquainted with some major fields within linguistics. Of course, there are many other branches, but that much is enough for our purpose here.

However, going back to the core of our topic, one may ask about the reasons why we teach English to our Arab students. One possible answer may be that we teach English because students have to learn it. But the question which still remains is why our students have to learn English. The answer to such a question may include the following points:

1. English is the first language in many countries in different parts of the world such as the United States of America, Canada, Britain, Australia, and New Zealand.

2. English is the second language in many countries such as India, Pakistan, and Nigeria.

3. English is the foreign language taught in many countries all over the world.

4. English is one of the language of advanced sciences.

5. It is one the languages needed to run a first-class business.

6. It is needed by students traveling abroad to start or continue their university learning.

In conclusion, English now, because of economics, political, and historical reasons, is almost an international language. It is nowadays one of the few languages needed in the fields of business, politics, and education. These reasons may be enough to answer the question why we teach and learn English.

1. 4. FLT Approaches:

In foreign language teaching (FLT), including teaching English as a foreign language (TEFL),there has been a lot of controversy concerning the best way to teach a foreign language. Different methodologists argue for different methods and approaches such as the grammar- translation approach, the direct approach, the aural-oral approach, and the eclectic one. A brief idea about each approach will be given in the following sections.

1. 4. 1. The Grammar-Translation Approach:

The grammar-translation approach is sometimes referred to in some books on teaching methods as the old method, the classical method, or the traditional method. The main features of this approach are these:

1. This approach emphasizes reading, writing, and translation rather than speech.

2. It uses the native language as a major means to explain the words and structures of the foreign language. *i.e.,* the target language.

3. It teaches grammatical rules or generalizations to control students' correct usage of the FL. *i.e.,* the foreign language.

4. It employs some kind of grammatical analysis of the FL sentences.

This approach has been criticized by some educators and linguist for neglecting the speaking skill, over-usage of the native language, over-emphases of the so-called rules of correctness, and for teaching about language instead of teaching language proper, i.e., language in use. However, these arguments against the traditional approach do not go without counter-arguments and the debate between proponents and opponents may actually continue without an end.

1. 4. 2. *The Direct Approach:*

The direct approach is an extreme reaction to the traditional approach. The main features of the direct approach are these:

1. The direct approach gives priority to speech.

2. It considers translation to be a useless or even harmful activity in teaching foreign languages.

3. The native language has no place in FLT.

4. Words and patterns of the FL are best taught through direct association with objects or situations.

5. No grammatical rules are used.

6. It uses the mim-mem method. i.e., mimicry and memorization, by which students memorize selected FL sentences, dialogues, and songs after imitation.

This approach, *i.e.,* the direct approach, has been criticized by some specialists for being the least direct approach. These critics argue that a really direct method should handle issues directly. The method, as it stands, avoids using the native language in explaining the meaning of FL words and structures. This avoidance leads into using time-wasting and roundabout techniques to achieve goals that can be better reached through time-saving and really direct means. In other word, which is more direct, to spend

about five minutes to explain a FL word through association and contextu-
alization without a full guarantee that it is comprehended or to give the
meaning in the native language in less than five seconds ? Of course, using
the native language is obviously more time-saving than the other technique.

1. 4. 3. The Aural-Oral Approach:

The aural-oral approach is another reaction to the old method and a
modification of the direct method. The aural-oral approach is sometimes
called the oral approach, the linguistics approach, the audio-lingual approach,
or the army method.

The assumption underlying the aural-oral approach are the following :

1. Language is mainly speech and writing is just a representation of
speech.

2. Speech is the FL skill that has to be emphasized more than reading or writing.

3. Teaching the FL should follow the order of listening, speaking,
reading, and then writing. This sequence implies that learners speak what
they have listened to, read what they have spoken, and write what or about
what they have read.

4. Acquiring the FL is similar to acquiring the native language.
5. The FL is best acquired through habit formation achieved by means
of pattern practice.

6.   Teaching about the FL is of no use.
7.   Each language is unique.
8.   Translation is harmful in teaching the FL.
9.   The best FL teacher is a trained native speaker of that FL.

However, all these assumptions are criticized and even refuted by
some methodologists who put forward these counter-arguments:

1. Speech is not the sole form language; it is just one form it.

2. Speech should not be emphasized at the expense of other FL skills, which are as important
as speech.

3. The order of listening, speaking, reading, and then writing is not essential because these skills may be taught simultaneously rather than sequentially.

4. FL acquisition is utterly different from native language acquisition in both qualitative and quantitative terms.

5. The FL is not learned through habit formation only, but through cognition as well.

6. Teaching about the FL is not without advantages.

7. It is true that languages are different, but they have some common features also.

8. Translation may be usefully employed in teaching the FL.

9. The native speaker of the FL may not the best teacher of that FL because he often does not know the students' native language and thus cannot predict or account for student's problems, mistakes, or areas of difficulty.

1. 4. 4. The Eclectic Approach:

The eclectic approach is a reaction to the previous three approaches. The assumptions underlying this eclectic approach are the following:

1. Each one of the three approaches has something to offer to the process of teaching foreign languages.

2. No approach is completely right or completely wrong since each approach has arguments for it and arguments against it.

3. The three approaches may supplement one another instead of contradicting or competing with one another.

4. No approach suits all goals, all students, all teachers, or all FL programs.

5. The important thing should be loyalty to students and not loyalty to a certain approach.

6. The teacher should feel free to use the best methods and techniques in any approach according to students' needs and the teaching-learning situation.

1. 5. Factors Influencing Methods:

There are many factors which may influence the methods used in teaching a foreign language. Teachers and educators need to be aware of these factors while designing and evaluating methods:

1. The teacher's training. Teachers with limited or no training on TFL methodology find it rather difficult to vary their methods.

2. The teacher's load. If the teacher is over-loaded with an excessive number of teaching hours and other school activities, he naturally tends to use methods that require minimal effort and, most probably, at the expense of efficiency.

3. The teacher's motivation. If the teacher is poorly motivated for one reason or another, his efficiency in teaching inevitably drops down.

4. The teacher's habituation. If a teacher has been accustomed to using a certain approach for several years, he usually resists the introduction of new methods unfamiliar to him.

5. The teacher's personality. Some teacher discover, through personal experience, that some methods of teaching fit them better than other methods because they go better with their own personality structure.

6. The teacher's learning. A teacher normally tends to teach a foreign language in a way similar to how he himself learned that FL.

7. Students' interest. If the class is interested in the FL, this gives the teacher more freedom to vary his methods.

8. Students' intelligence. Studies have shown that there is a positive correlation between intelligence and FL learning. Therefore, teaching bright students certainly differs from teaching slow students.

9. Students' age. Teaching children differs from teaching adolescents or adults. As the child moves to adolescence and later to adulthood, his readiness for imitation gradually gives place to his preference for intellectualizing.

10. Students' expectations. What students expect from a FL course may affect the teacher's methods. These expectations are determined by their previous experience with former FL courses, their actual needs, study habits, and general learning strategies.

11. FL-NL relationship. If the foreign language (FL) and the native language (NL) are different in all aspects, the problems are different from those in another situation where the two languages are different in some aspects only.

12. Duration. If the FL program is planned to continue for a limited time, the goals of such a program are usually limited in scope. On the other hand, if the program is a long one, its goals are usually wider. When goals are different, they entail some differences in methods.

13. Facilities. FLT methods are influenced by the existence or absence of facilities such as pictures, tapes, films, laboratories, and radio programs.

14. Goals. Is the goal teach speaking, reading, writing, some or all of these skills ? The answer, of course, determines what methods to use.

15. Tests. Teachers and students tend to emphasize what tests emphasize. If tests neglect a certain aspect of language, teachers and students usually neglect that aspect. If tests emphasize the productive aspect of language, FLT methods may differ from those used in a situation where tests emphasize recognition.

16. Class size. Methods successful with small classes may not be equally so with large classes.

One implication of these factors is that the teacher should be psychologically and professionally prepared to vary or at least modify his methods to suit different educational situations. It will be exhausting, unfruitful, unfair, or unwise if the teacher blindly and habitually insists on utilizing one single method in all situations.

Another implication of these factors is related to method designers and evaluators, who should take into consideration the practical factors which may interfere in the actual process of teaching such as the teacher's load and training. Some practical factors may work against a certain method in application. The solution in this case is either to tolerate a slight modification of the method so as to cope with those practical factors or to overcome any negative factors so as to render that method applicable.

1. 6. Program Types:

There are two distinct types of FL programs. The first one is the school program, where the FL is taught like any other school subject. For example, English is taught at intermediate and secondary school in the Arab countries for about forty minutes every day on the average.

The second type of FL programs is the intensive one. Here the foreign language (FL) is taught as the only subject to a special group of learners for a period ranging from a week to eighteen months.

Of course, there are fundamental differences between those tow types of programs:

1. FL hour. The time devoted for FL teaching in an intensive program is much more than the FL time in a school program. For example, if an intensive program gives eight hours of FL teaching per day for a year, this will be quantitatively equivalent to twenty years of FLT in a school program.

2.   Goals. The FLT school program usually has a variety of goals related to all language skills : listening, speaking, reading, and writing. On the other hand, intensive programs often focus on a narrow rang of objectives for special purposes.

3. Motivation. In many school programs all over the world, the FL course is obligatory for every student or, in some cases, the student may choose the FL he prefers to learn from other available FL courses. But, in intensive courses, it is often the case that the learner himself chooses to take the intensive course or not. Of course, this implies that learners in an intensive GL course are on the whole internally motivated than learners in a school FL program.

4. Age. In a school FL program, learners are generally between six and eighteen years of age. In an intensive course, they are usually adults who are clear on their plans and goals.

1. 7. Effective Teaching :

One main aim of training teachers is to familiarize them with effective methods of teaching, which guarantee maximal learning. This book achieves this aim through the following:

1.   Teachers are guided how to teach the pronunciation of the FL, which is English in our case.

2.   They are guided how to teach the grammatical structures of the FL.

3.   They are instructed on how to teach FL vocabulary.

4.   They are also instructed on how to teach FL reading.

5.   They are advised on how to teach writing.

6.   They are also advised on how to test each language skill.

7.   They are advised on what aids they can use.

However, effective teaching is not secured through knowing how to teach only, but through other means as well:

1. The teacher must maintain a good appearance because he will be looked at as an example and surveyed from head to foot by scores of students' examining eyes.

2. The teacher's voice must be clear and loud enough to be easily heard by all students in the classroom. Otherwise, students will find it dif-ficult to follow what he says and, in consequence, their attention wanes.

3. The teacher should prepare his lesson very well in respect of what and how he is going to teach.

4. He should master his subject matter and know more than his students do and more than what textbooks offer.

5. He should encourage his students through praise, rewards, and the like.

6. He should notice individual differences among students.

7. He should be kind to his students.

8. Kindness should not mean weakness since the teacher needs to be kind and strict at the same time.

9. The teacher should be fair to all his students. He has to treat them equally without any prejudice for or against any of them.

10. He should like his work because his students can easily tell whether he really likes his profession or not and their attitude may largely depend on their conclusion.

11. He should give his students the maximal chance to participate in class activities.

12. He should know not only what to teach, but also the different methods of teaching.

In fact, teachers are required and urged to learn how to teach as effectively as possible for several reasons:

1. An effective teacher is a happy person because effectiveness leads to success, which in turn secures self-satisfaction.

2. Effective teaching is one step towards optimal learning. If a teacher teaches well, students often learn well.

3. Effective teaching implies minimal waste of time and effort on the part of students and teachers because the teacher in this case selects those methods which lead to best results with time-and-effort economy.

4. Effective teaching is often accompanied not only by good learning, but also by happy learning because effective teaching involves motivation, variation, aids, social warmth, and similar factors that make learning a pleas- ant experience to students.

1. 8. Discussion

1. Give two other definitions of language offered by encyclopedias or other references and comment on them.

2. Give some more branches of linguistics not mentioned in this chapter.
3. What are other reasons for learning English as a foreign language ?

4. What are the positive and negative points of each FLT approach?
5. Which FLT approach do you find most suitable ?

6. Some say that the direct approach is the least direct one. Com-ment on this statement.

7. What arguments can you think against the assumptions of the oral approach ?

8. What is the implication of the existence of factors influencing FLT methods ?
9. Elaborate on each of the qualities of a good teacher.

TEACHING PRONUNCIATION

One area in FLT which requires special attention is how to overcome the difficulties of FL pronunciation. The starting point in this aspect is knowing the FL sounds and how they differ from the native-language sounds and what problems are caused by these difference between the sound systems of the two languages.

Such contrastive knowledge of the sound systems of Arabic, the NL in this case, and English, the FL, is helpful to the teacher in several ways:

1. The teacher gets acquainted with those sounds that exist in English but do not exit in Arabic.

2. He also gets familiar with those sounds that exist in Arabic but do not exist in English.

3. The teacher is helped to know how each FL sound is articulated in the human vocal system.

4. This contrastive knowledge of the NL and FL sound systems enables the teacher to pinpoint problem areas predict problems before they happen.

5. When a pronunciation problem occurs, the teacher will not be astonished by its occurrence. On the contrary, such a problem will not only be expected, but also easily accounted for. In other words, the teacher will be able to know which FL sounds will be problematic to his students and which NL sounds will be transferred into the learning situation. Further, the teacher will

be able to explain why a certain FL sound is no problem whereas another FL sound is a problem.

6. This knowledge of problem areas in FL pronunciation and of sound articulation makes the teacher abler to handle such problems more successfully.

II. 1. English Components:

Each sound system of any language can be classified into segmental phonemes and superasegmental phonemes. Segmental phonemes include consonants and vowels and suprasegmentals include stresses, pitches, and terminals.

As for English, it has twenty-four consonants or consonantal phonemes, each of which is given a symbol between two slashes, an example in its normal graphic form, a description of voice or voicelessness, its point of articulation and finally its manner of articulation. The English consonants are the following:

1. /p/, pen, voiceless, bilabial,   stop
2. /b/, bit, voiced, bilabial,   stop
3. /t/, ten, voiceless, alveolar,   stop
4. /d/, day, voiced, alveolar,   stop
5. /k/, kill, voiceless, velar,   stop
6. /g/, good, voiced, velar,   stop
7. /Ć/, chair, voiceless, alveopalatal,   affricate
8. /j/, jam, voiced, alveopatal,   affricate
9. /f/, fine, voiceless, labiodental,   fricative
10. /v/, vine, voiced, labiodental,   fricative
11. /θ/, thin, voiceless, dental,   fricative
12. /ð/, the, voiced, dental,   fricative
13. /s/, sea, voiceless, alveolar,   fricative
14. /z/, zero, voiced, alveolar,   fricative
15. /š/, shine, voiceless, alveopalatal,   fricative
16. /ž/, treasure, voiced, alveopatal,   fricative
17. /h/, hen, voiceless, glottal,   fricative
18. /l/, lay, voiced, alveolar,   lateral

19. /m/, man, voiced, bilabial,   nasal

20. /n/, now, voiced, alveolar,   nasal

21. / η /, sing, voiced, velar,   nasal

22. /w/, win, voiced, bilabial,   semivowel

23. /r/, rain, voiced, alveolar,   semivowel

24. /y/, yet, voiced, alveopalatal,   semivowel

For students who have not taken courses on phonetics, brief definitions of phonetic terms used in the previous description may be needed:

1. Voiced : accompanied with the vibration of the vocal cords in the glottis, e.g., /d/.

2. Voiceless : accompanied with no such vibration, e.g., /t/.

3. Bilabial : produced by the upper and lower lips, e.g., /m/.

4. Labiodental : produced by the lower lip and the upper teeth. e.g., /v/.

5. Dental : produced by the tip of the tongue and the upper teeth. e.g., / θ /.

6. Alveolar : the tip (apex) of the tongue touches the inner upper gum, e.g., /t/.

7. Velar : produced by the back (dorsum) of the tongue and the velum (soft palate), e.g., /k/.

8. Aleveopalatal : produced by the front of the tongue and the front of the palate, e.g., /s/.

9. Stop : a sound produced by stopping the breath stream somewhere in the vocal system, e.g., /p/.

10. Fricative : a sound produced by letting the breath stream go through a narrowed passage, e.g., /f/.

11. Affricative : a combination of a stop and a fricative, e.g., / Ć /.

12. Lateral : a sound produced by letting the breath stream pass through one or two sides of the month, e.g., /I/.

13. Nasal : a sound produced by the closure of the oral cavity, i.e.,

the mouth, and the opening of the nasal cavity, *i.e.*, the nose, e.g., /n/.

14. Semi-vowel : a sound produced like a vowel but distributed like a consonant, e.g., /w/.

11. 2. *English Vowels* :

The vowels in English constitute one of the most controversial areas in linguistics owing to differences among phoneticians, dialects, idiolects, and transcription systems. Since this is a book on methods and not on phonetics, it suffices to mention only what is necessary for a teacher of English.

There are nine simple vowels in English, all of which are voiced. Their quality and description are determined by the position of the highest part of the tongue in the mouth. These simple vowels are included in the following list:

1. /i/, bit, unrounded, high, front
2. /e/, bet, unrounded, mid, front
3. /æ/, bat, unrounded, low, front
4. /i/, just, unrounded, high, central
5. /a/, but, unrounded, mid, central
6. /a/, dog, unrounded, low, central
7. /u/, put, rounded, high, back
8. /o/, boat, rounded, mid, back
9. /ɔ/, bought, rounded, low, back

This list includes some terms which may need some explanation:

1. rounded: produced with the lips rounded, e.g., /u/.

2. unrounded: produced without rounding the lips, e.g., /e/.

3. high, mid, low: up-down position of the tongue in the mouth.

4. front, central, back: forward-backward positions of the tongue in the mouth.

However, these nine vowels are just the simple ones. One can list twenty seven complex vowels more by combining each simple vowel with each of the three glides or semi-vowels: /r/, /w/, and /y/. For more details on this subject, one may consult specializes references on phonetics.

11. 3. English Stress:

As was mentioned before, consonants and vowels are called segmental phonemes or segmental because speech can be segmented into those consecutive components. On the other hand, stresses, terminals, and pitches are called supersegmental phonemes or supersegmentals because they are superimposed on those segmentals. In the following sections, we shall discuss the different types of stress: word stress, sentence stress, and contrastive stress.

11. 3. 1. Word Stress:

Each syllable in a word has a peak or nucleus, which corresponds to the vowel of that syllable. Each syllable nucleus receives a certain degree of stress which varies from one syllable to another within the same word.

In English, there are four degrees of stress:

1. primary stress : it is the strongest one and symbolized by/ ′/.

2. secondary stress : it is next in strength and symbolizes by /^/.

3. tertiary stress : it is weaker than secondary stress and symbolized by /ˋ /.

4. weak stress : it is the weakest stress and symbolized by /ˇ/.

However, the important degree of stress in word pronunciation is the primary one. In fact, most dictionaries present two levels of stress : stress and no stress. In this sense, stress refers to the primary level and no stress refers to the absence of primary stress or, in other words, the presence of nay of the other three stress levels. Of course, such dichotomy is used because it is those two levels which are actually needed for practical purposes.

As a matter of fact, FL students usually make a lot of mistakes in placing the right stress in the right position partly because stress distribution in the NL differs from its distribution in the FL. Further, word stress in English does not follow regular patterns. However, there are some hints on stress which deal with some groups of words and which may be helpful in learning and controlling stress behavior:

1. A word ending in-*ate* has a primary stress on the third syllable from the end, e.g., *illustrate*, *anticipate*, and *hesitate*.

2. A word ending in *–ic, -ion, -ious,-ian*, or–*ial* receives a primary stress on the second syllable from the end, e.g., *domestic, opinion, religious, politi-cian,* and *artificial.*

3. A word of four syllables or more receives a primary stress on the third syllable from the end, e.g., *probability, economy,* and *political.*

4. A word of two syllables that can function as a verb and a noun with a prefix receives a primary stress on the second syllable, e.g., *demand, request,* and *respect.*

5. Some two-syllable words receive stress on the first syllable when they are nouns and on the second when they are verbs, e.g., *insult, record, object, export,* and *import.*

6. Compound nouns usually have stress on the first component word, e.g., *blackboard, football,* and *classroom.*

These generalizations cover a small percentage of English words. The rest of English words are to be learned through imitation and practice
because their stress distribution is quite irregular. Even those words
covered by the mentioned generalizations cannot be learned intellectually regarding their stress
. in fact, practice is essential in all cases in order to master stress pronunciation. However, those generalizations on stress distribution function as supporters of practice, aids to memory, and refe-rences in cases of doubt.

---

11. 3. 2. Sentence Stress :

When a word is spoken in isolation, one of its syllables, and one only, takes the primary stress. On the other hand, when words are put together to form an utterance, i.e., a speech unit bounded by silence, only one word in that utterance receives a primary stress. This stressed word is usually the most important word in the speech unit, which may be a sentence or a part of a sentence, e.g., he read the paper quickly. In this example, each word in isolation, takes a primary stress, but when the words are strung together in one sentence, only the last word takes the primary stress.

As a matter fact, sentence stress and its distribution may form a
rather complicated area. However, for the sake of practically and simplify- cation, related facts may be summarized in the following:

1. Nominals take secondary or primary stresses.

2. Adjectivals take secondary stresses.

3. Verbals may take any stress.

4. Prepositionals take tertiary or weak stresses.

5. Conjunctionals take tertiary or weak stresses.

6. Auxiliaries take weak stresses.

7. The emphatic do takes a primary stress.

8.   Pronouns take tertiary or weak stresses.
By examining these generalizations on sentence stress, one may notice that there is a positive correlation between the word importance and its
stress level: the more important a word is, the stronger its stress is. Be-
sides, these generalizations apply to sentences pronounced normally. One
may also notice that content words take primary or secondary stresses,
whereas grammatical words take tertiary or weak stresses.

To help learners catch sentence stress, the teacher is advised to do
the following :

1. Expose students to the FL as spoken by its native speakers through recordings.
2. Let them respect after you during model reading.
3. Speak at normal speed and encourage your students to do the same in order not to distort
sentence intonation by excessively slow enunciation.

11. 3. 3. Contrastive Stress :

The speaker may wish to emphasize a certain word in his sentence. Such emphasis is expressed by giving this word a primary stress. For example in a sentence like *He ate tow apples*, the speaker has the following choices:

1. He may stress the word *he* to mean that *he* and not *she* or *they* did the eating.

2. He may stress the word *ate* to mean that he ate and not gave or bought them. In other words, this stress emphasizes the action itself.

3. He may stress the word *two* to mean that he ate two and not one or three.

27

4. He may stress the word « apples » , which is the normal way of saying the sentence.

II. 4. English Junctionres :

There are four types of junctures in English:

1. /+/ is called the plus juncture or the internal juncture. It appears between a secondary stress and a primary one, e.g., blâck /+/ bird. This juncture has a phonetic effect on the preceding phone and the following one.

2. /→/ is called the sustained external juncture or sustained terminal, which is equivalent to a comma in writing. It cases some prolongation in the preceding syllable, e.g., *the letter I had* → *is his.*
This terminal is a short pause that occurs during speaking or reading.

3. /↘/is called the falling juncture or the fading juncture. It is a rapid passing away of voice into silence, e.g., *he could understand quickly* ↘

4. /↗/ is called the rising juncture. It is a rapid, sudden, and short rise in pitch, e.g., can you explain the reason for that ↗?

II. 5. English Pitches :

Pitch is the tone of voice, which has four degrees in English:

1. Pitch /1/. It is called the low pitch, which marks the end of a statement or a wh-question. It is usually accompanied with the falling juncture, e.g., *he came yesterday*[1]↘ .

2. Pitch /2/. It is called the normal pitch, which usually marks the beginning or continuity of speech, e.g., [2]*the good soldier* [2]→*obeys his superiors*[1] ↘ .Besides, this normal pitch, if it marks continuity, is accompanied with the sustained juncture as the given example shows.

3. Pitch /3/. It is called the high pitch, which usually marks the end of a yes-no question, e.g., *can you do it*[3] ↗.In this case, it is accompanied with the rising juncture. Further, the high pitch is usually superimposed on the stressed syllable at the end of or near the end of the sentence, e.g.,[2]*he* [3]*conquered them*[1]↘ .

4. Pitch/4/. It is called the extra high pitch, which is used to make emphasis or express surprise.

II. 6. English Intonation :

Those pitches and junctures are combined together in different ways to vary the intonation of English sentences. These combinations make two common patterns of intonation distributed as follows:

1. /232 ↘/. This pattern marks the intonation of statements, e.g.,

³he went to ³school ¹ ↘ .

2. /231 ↘/. It also the intonation of wh-questions, i.e., questions beginning with words like who, what, where, when, all of which begin with the letters *wh-*, e.g., 3what have you ³*done*¹ ↘? This means that the pattern /231 ↘/ is the commonest one because it marks statements and wh-questions.

3. /231 ↗/. This pattern ends up with a high pitch and a rising terminal. Such a pattern is used with yes-no questions, which begin with an auxiliary and require an answer which starts with yes or no, e.g., ³*did he go to* ³*school*³ ↗?

Concerning the teaching of superasegmentals, which include stresses, pitches, and junctures, there is no other way to teach them than imitation and practice. The teacher gives the correct model in all cases and asks students to repeat in chorus, in groups, and then individually. This applies to teaching words and grammatical structures as well.

II. 7. English-Arabic Contrast :

The basic problem in teaching FL pronunciation result from the dif- ferences in the sound systems of the FL and the NL, i.e., English and Arabic in this case. If the teacher knows these differences, he can predict diffi- culties and most probably handle them efficiently.

Actually, English-Arabic phonemic contrast can be a very long subject, but here it suffices to mention the most prominent areas of contrast:

1. /p/ is a phoneme in English but it is merely a variety or an allophone of /b/ in Arabic.

2. /t/ is alveolar in English but dental in Arabic.

3. /d/ is alveolar in English but dental in Arabic.

4. /č/ is a phoneme in English, but it is an allophone of /k/ in some dialects of Arabic and does not exist in standard Arabic.

5. /v/ is a phoneme in English, but it does not exist in Arabic.

6. /ž/ is a phoneme in English, but an allophone of /j/ in some Arab dialects.

7. /ŋ/ is a phoneme in English, but has no existence in Arabic.

8. /e/ exists in English but not in Arabic.

9. /ɨ/ exists in English but not in Arabic.

10. /ɔ/ is an English phoneme but does not exist in Arabic.

11. /r/ is flat in British English and a retroflex in American English but it is a trill in Arabic.

12. In English, two or more consonants may cluster together in the same syllable, but in Arabic this cannot occur, e.g., *street, sixty.*

The teacher of English should expect that his students will find difficulty with the previously-mentioned English sounds. Arab students confuse

/p/ with /b/, / ć / with /j/,/ž/ with/š/, / ŋ /with /n/ and /g/, /e/ with /i/, /ɨ/ with /i/, and /ɔ/ with /o/. Besides, they may produce English
/r/ as a trill and not as a retroflex. They may also introduce a vowel before or inside a consonantal cluster to separate consonants.

II. 8. Transfer of Learning :

In Arab schools, English is usually taught at the beginning of the inter- mediat stage to twelve-year-old students. This means that the FL learner
has already mastered his NL, Arabic, including its sound system. As a
result, this learner carries into the FL class all the sound habits associated with Arabic.

Some of the NL habits may facilitate learning the FL. In this case, transfer of learning entails some kind of facilitation. On the other hand,
some NL habits may interfere in learning the FL. In this case, transfer
of learning leads to inhibition.

In other words, similarities between the NL and the FL normally facili- tate learning the FL and such transfer of previous learning has a positive effect. In contrast, differences between the NL and the FL normally inhabit learning the FL and thus the result in a transfer of a negative effect.

Therefore, it is necessary for the teacher to know the areas of similarity and those of differences between the FL and the NL. This knowledge enables the teacher to predict, account for, and overcome any pronunciation problems met by students and caused by the negative transfer of NL habits.

II. 9. Presentation and Practice :

In the previous sections, we have given a brief description of the sound system of English and how it contrasts with Arabic and we have then located some problem areas in pronunciation. In the following sections, we shall deal with how to overcome such problems and how to conduct pronunciation drills. In addition, we shall present some related concapts.

II. 9. 1. Phonetics and Phonemic Differences :

The phonological differences between tow utterances may be phonetic or phonemic. A phonetic difference is that which causes no difference in meaning. For example, if the word tip is pronounced with aspiration on the last sound or without aspiration, the meaning of the word is not influenced by this variation in pronunciation

On the other hand, a phonemic difference is that which is accom panied with a difference in meaning. For example the difference between bill and pill is phonemic because the difference between /b/ and /p/ has caused a difference in meaning.

In teaching the FL at schools, what actually matters at such a level is the phonemic difference and not the phonetic one. The latter becomes important when the FL is taught at very advanced levels and for special purposes.

II. 9. 2. Minimal Pairs :

Those phonemic differences are best expressed through minimal pairs. A minimal pair is two words differing in one sound or phoneme contrasting in similar positions and resulting in a semantic difference. The best way to clarify this concept may be a list of examples phonemically transcribed:

/fin/   /fig/

```
/pen/      /ten/
/lip/      /tip/
/til/      /tel/
```

The involved contrast between the two words of the minimal pair is
a contrast in a sound and not in writing. In other words, the contrast is a phonemic one, rather than a graphic or phonetic one.

In fact, the concept of a nominal pair leads to another important con- cept, which is the phoneme. The phoneme is a class of sounds phonetically similar and in complementary distribution or free variation. The member
sounds of this class are called allophones.

To clarify the concept of a phoneme, let us see this example. The
/p/ in /pin/, /spin/,and /tip/ is produced a bit differently in each word.
It is aspirated in /pin/, unaspirated in /spin/, and unreleased in /tip/.
To put it differently, of /p/ occurs initially it is aspirated. If /p/ occurs after /s/, it is unaspirated. If /p/ occurs finally, it is unreleased.

This example shows that /p/ as a phoneme has three varieties, each of which is used in a certain environment where other varieties cannot
occur. This explain the concept of the«complementary distribution» of allophones.

Moreover, when /p/ is final, it is either unreleased or aspirated. In other words, the speaker is free to aspirate or unreleased it. This explains the concept of the free variation of allophones in the same environment.

> ## II. 9. 3. Pronunciation Drills:

The teacher should be able to construct drills of his own, and in some cases, on the spur of the moment, to teach his students or remedy their pronunciation problems. These drills may be made according to these guidelines :

1. Minimal pairs are effective particularly in showing students how
a phoneme contrasts with another and how each phoneme causes a diffe- rence in meaning.

2. The minimal pair should start with the easy phoneme followed
by the difficult one. In the case of Arab students, /b/ should come before /p/, /i/ before /e/, /o/

before /ɔ/, and so on.

3. The pronunciation drills starts with minimal pairs followed by phrases and then sentences. The phrases are of three types presented in this order : the first type includes the easy phoneme, the second the dif- ficult phoneme, and the third the two phonemes mixed in the same phrase. The same order applies to sentences.

4. The teacher gives the model pronunciation and then students repeat what he has said.

5. Students' repletion usually goes in this sequence : the whole class, groups, and then individuals. In other words, we start with chorus repetition followed by group repetition and finally individual repetition.

6. Recognition should precede production. This means that before students are asked to produce a difficult sound, they should be trained to recognize it when heard with other sounds. If the problem is /i/ end /e/, for instance, /i/ is given number 1 and /e/ is given number 2. then the teacher pronounces words containing either /i/ or /e/ and students are required to say one whenever they hear a word with /i/ and two whenever they hear a word with /e/.

II. 9. 4. Signals :

Pronunciation drills as any other oral drills usually proceed fairly quickly. Therefore, the teacher needs to use some techniques that help him conduct such drills easily and efficiently. For example, he can use his hands to signal the beginning or the end of students' repetition. Further, he can use hand signals to specify who to repeat : the whole class, a certain group, or individuals.

Through signaling, the teacher can save time and effort. He can also conduct drills easily. Besides, he avoids confusing the class by using hand signals instead of oral instructions, which may be wrongly taken by some students to be models for repetition.

II. 9. 5. Props :

In teaching pronunciation, the teacher may use mirrors to help stu- dents see the points or manners of articulation of some sounds. He may use certain pictures of the vocal apparatus to demonstrate the function of some vocal organs in producing some sounds. He may also draw some explanatory diagrams on the chalkboard or on special charts.

II. 9. 6. Partials :

If a sentence is too long for a student or a group of students to repeat, the teacher may shorten it through dividing it in a process called build-
back formation . The teacher starts from the very end of the sentence
adding one word or more each time till the student becomes able to repeat the whole sentence. The purpose of going backward rather than forward
in building up the sentence is to retain the same intonation.

II. 10. Special Problems :

This section will try to offer some help concerning the pronunciation
of some common suffixes that are often problematic to the learners of
English as a foreign language, e.g., the plural endings that are suffixed to nouns, the present endings suffixed to verbs with third person singular subjects, and the past endings suffixed to make the past form of a verb.
It is infrequent to find a sentence that does not have one or more of those suffixes that express plurality, past tense, or some kind of subject-verb concord. Because of this high frequency of their occurrence and, conse- quently, a high probability of mispronunciation, these suffixes need special attention on the teacher's part.

II. 10 . 1. The Plural Morpheme :

To begin with, the morpheme may be defined as the smallest mean- ingful uinit. For example, the word improbability consists of three morphemes   : in+probable+ity. Each unit of these three is a morpheme because it has a distinct meaning and because each unit is indivisible to smaller units.

On the other hand, the word *boy* is only one morpheme because it cannot be divided into any smaller units that are meaningful. However, the word *boy* may be considered as having two morphemes: boy+zero, which marks singu- larity.

Now, after getting acquainted with the morpheme concept, let us examine these three groups of nouns with regular plurals :

Group [1]	Group [2]	Group [3]
watch	cat	dog
brush	book	school
bus	top	friend

34

To pluralize the words in Group [1], we add the sound /ɪz/.The plurals in Group [2] are formed by adding the phoneme /s/. The plurals in Group [3] are formed by adding the phoneme /z/.

The underlying generalizations may be stated as follows :

1. If the final sound of the singular noun is a hissing sound, i.e., /s/, /č/,/ĵ/,/š/, or/z/, the plural morpheme is /ɪz/.

2. If the final sound is voiceless, the plural morpheme is pronounced /s/.

3.   If the final sound is voiced, the plural morpheme is pronounced /z/.

Therefore, it can be said that the plural morpheme has at least three phonemic varieties conditional by phonetic pre-environments. Each variety
is called an allomorph.

Mispronunciation in these cases is usually caused by misleading
graphic units, i.e., letters. Although both of the words *books* and *dogs* end in the same letter, i.e., s, this s is pronounced differently in each case:/s/ and /z/ respectively. Even in the case of brushes and other words ending in *es*, this *es* sometimes leads to a mispronunciation : the s in

es not /s/ but /z/ and es is thus / ɪz/ and not /ɪs/.

II. 10. 2. *The Present Morpheme* :

The present morpheme refers to the morpheme that is suffixed to the verb in the present simple tense when the subject is a third person singular, e.g., he, she, it, John, the girl, a car, etc.
The pronunciation generalizations on this morpheme are the same as those on the plural morpheme.
To check this, let us look at these three groups of verbs :

Group (1)	Group (2)	Group (3)
modernize	look	need
wish	let	weaken
practise	peep	swim

The first group takes / ɪz/ because each verb ends is a hissing sound. The second group takes /s/ because each verb ends in a voiceless phone-me. The third group takes the allomorph /z/ because each verb ends in voiced phoneme. This implies that the present morpheme has three distinct

35

allomorphs conditioned by phonetic environments.

II. 10. 3. The Past Morpheme :

The past morpheme is added to the infinitive to make the past form
of the verb. For illustration, let us have a look at these three groups of regular verbs :

Group (1)	Group (2)	Group (3)
want	wish	kill
need	kick	clean
hesitate	pass	disturb

The past of Group 1 verbs is formed by adding / ɨd/. The past of Group 2 verbs is formed by
added /t/. the past of Group 3 verbs is formed by adding /d/. Notice that slashed mark sounds
and not letters.

The derived generalizations on the distribution of such varieties may be summarized as
follows :

1. If the final is /t/ or /d/, we add / ɨd/.

2. If the final is voiceless, we add /t/.

3. If the final is voiced, we add /d/.

This means that the past morpheme has three varieties, i.e., allo- morphs, conditioned by
preceding phonetic environments. But we have to remember that past allomorphs are three if
we consider regular verbs only.
If we are to include all verbs whether regular or irregular, such allomorphs will be much more
than three.

To conclude, the teacher is expected to be aware of the varieties of plural, past, and present
morphemes and how each variety is pronounced
and in what environments. In fact, such awareness is necessary owing to
the high frequency of these morphemes, which exist in almost every
sentence. In addition, these morphemes are unfortunately often mis- pronounced by teachers,
students and student teachers. The common
related mistakes may be the following:

1. The grapheme *s* in words like *dogs* is mispronounced as /s/ instead of /z/. To account for
this mistake, *s* is inconsistent in its pronunciation :it may be /s/ or /z/. Therefore, such a
mistake may be due to overstretched analogy.

2. Some learners mispronounce *es* in words like *churches* as /s/,/z/ or/ ǂs/ instead of / ǂz/ owing to erroneous analogy as well.

3. Some mispronounce *ed* as /d/ or / ǂd/ instead of /t/ in words like *wished*.

One reason underlying such mistakes in pronunciation may be being misled by the written form of the word, which does not always correspond
to the phonemic form.

II. 10. 4. *American-British Differences* :

The teacher had better to know the differences between American English and British English. Of course, there are differences not only in pronun- ciation, but in some grammatical structures and some vocabulary items
also, in addition, there are differences within American English, *i.e.*, among American dialects. Further, there are differences within British English, *i.e.*, among British dialects. What concerns us here is only the question of those differences in pronunciation between British English (or English English, as some like to call it) and American English to the exclusion of differences in other areas.

Here are the major differences in pronunciation:

1. Before a voiceless fricative and occasionally /n/, British /a/ is American /æ/, e.g., *calf, patch, pass, aunt.*

2. The British /r/ is usually pronounced with a flat tongue and hence we have the r-less dialect. The American /r/ is usually a retroflex.

3. The British /ɔ/ is often an American /a/, e.g., *cot, dog, hot.*

4. The intervocalic British /t/ is usually an American flap /t/, e.g., *letter, water.*

5. The British intonation descends gradually from the beginning of
the sentence till the end. On the other hand, the American intonation main- tains a rather level tone until just before the termination of the utterance where it rises up and then down or up again.

6. The British rang between the highest and lowest pitches is wider than the American range, which causes the British English to seen a little more emotional.

These main differences should be clear to the teacher and his attitude should be acceptance of both dialects when used by his students.

However, it is generally better if he himself can use one dialect consis- tently.

II. 11. Minimizing Difficulties :

Here are some suggestions for teachers that may help them to mini- mize their students' pronunciation difficulties:

1. students should listen to new words before they produce them
orally. The underlying educational principle is that perception and listening should precede production and speaking.

2. The teacher should always give his students the correct pronun-
ciation of new words because he is a model fully imitated by learners. This requires that the teacher has to check the pronunciation of most words, if
not all .It is easier to teach afresh than to re-teach after wrong learning.

3. The teacher has to pay attention to suprasegmentals as well as segmentals. This implies that he has to pronounce words correctly regarding their consonants, vowels and stress.

4. The teacher has to pronounce sentences with their correct intonation and sentence stress and at a fairly normal speed.

5. Good pronunciation should be aimed at even when one is teaching other skills such as reading aloud, grammatical structures, and voca- bulary.

6. The teacher should call his students' attention to silent letters
while teaching new words by probably dotting them when demonstrated
on the chalkboard. Such focusing is helpful in learning both pronunciation
and spelling.

7. The teacher has to emphasize words with problem sounds more
than words devoid of such sounds. The former words require more repeti- tion.

8. The teacher has to design pronunciation drills that handle some common pronunciation difficulties especially those caused by new sounds
not existing in the native language.

9. The teacher may teach his students some regularities that con-
troll the relationship between writing and pronunciation, e.g., the pattern of hide, bite and site and the pattern of hid, bit, and sit. These grapheme-pho-

neme generalizations facilitate learning through moving from the general
to the specific.

II. 12. Discussion :

1. What are the members of each following class : segmentals, superasegmentals, stops, fricatives, nasals, semivowels, and short vowels
in the English language ?

2. What are the differences among word tress, sentence stress, and contrastive stress ? Give examples.

3. What sounds exist in English but do not exist in Arabic?

4. What sounds exist in Arabic but not in English ?

5. What is the effect of learning transfer on teaching foreign lan- gauges ?

6. Give fifty minimal pairs with five pairs on each pair of sounds.

7. Give sixty plural nouns classified into three groups with each
group exemplifying an allomorph of the plural morpheme.

8. Design a model pronunciation drill on any problem sound you choose.

9. Give sixty verbs in three groups to exemplify the allomorphs of
the present morpheme.

10. Give sixty verbs in three groups to show the three varieties of the past morpheme.

11. List ten more examples on each of the first four differences
between British English and American English.

12. How else can pronunciation difficulties be overcome ?

TEACHING GRAMMAR

111. 1. Definitions of Grammar:

The term grammar has been used by different people to mean different things :

1. Some used *grammar* as a term to refer to a group of rules that instruct learners, speakers, and writers on what to say and what not to say or what is right and what is wrong. With this meaning, grammar takes a prescriptive role.

2. Some used the term *grammar* to refer to a set of summarizing generalizations on the existent behavior of language. With this meaning, grammar takes merely a descriptive role.

3. Some used the term *grammar* to mean a theory on the structure of language, a book on grammar, or a teaching lesson where grammar is focused on.

In this book, the term *grammar* will be used with the second meaning in mind. This meaning implies that grammar is nothing more than a record of language habits at a certain period of time. Such implication is obviously in line with the view of structuralizes, who hold that grammarians are not, nor have they to be, guardians of linguistic correctness.

111. 2. Grammar Theories:

There have been several theories on grammar. The following sections Will give just a brief account of the main theories and show how each

theory may affect methodology. For details concerning grammar theoriza-
tion, one may consult references on pure linguistics.

111. 2. 1. Traditional Grammar :

Traditional grammar generally tended to be prescriptive by trying to impose some rules of language correctness and so to protect language form so-called corruption and impurity. To put it differently, traditional grammar
had the tendency to plan for language instead of just reporting how it actually goes.

Traditional grammarians established the famous eight parts of
speech : verb, adverb, noun, pronoun, adjective, preposition, conjunction,
and interjection. This classification has often been criticized by neo-gram-
marians for inconsistency and inaccuracy :some definitions do not define
well because they do not exclude members of other classes: some definitions are based on semantic considerations whereas others are based on
functional ones, which means that there is no unified criterion for defin-
ing or classifying. However, there may be no room here to argue for or
against these points because the focus of this book is methods of teaching.

Further, traditional grammar employs parsing, which is a categoriza-
tion of words within a certain sentence into subject, object, verb, direct
object, indirect object, complement, and so on.

This type of grammar, i.e., traditional grammar, may be helpful in
teaching foreign languages owing to its relative simplicity, practicality,
and usefulness. Its eight parts of speech plus functional categories with
the so-called rules have proved to be pedagogically beneficial despite the
criticism of some modern linguist against this grammar.

In addition, when a traditional grammarian gives the rules of a language, let the teacher look at those rules as guides to students and not as
superimposed instructions on how a group of people ought to use that
language. Further, the need for rules by foreign-language learners is certainly more urgent than the need of native speakers. The learners of
foreign languages often express their satisfaction with knowing the patterns and regularities of the target language because such generalizations
make the learned material controllable and retainable.

III. 2. 2. Immediate-Constituent Grammar:

Immediate constituent (IC) grammar is absolutely description and has nothing to do with how a language should be. Its main concern is to ana- lyse sentences as they actually are.

The IC theory assumes that every English sentence can be divided into tow units, each of which can be divided into further two. This process of bi-division is to continue till the word level is reached, where no more cutting can be carried on.

In teaching a foreign language, the teacher may make use of this grammar by substituting one unit for two units and by repeated substitu- tion until the sentence is reduced to its tow minimal components, i.e., sub- ject and predicate. Of course, this depends on the students' level and on how much the teacher himself knows of this grammar theory and on how intelligently he can apply his theoretical knowledge for practical and edu- cational objectives.

III. 2. 3. Tagmemic Grammar :

According to the tagmemic theory, i.e., tagmemics, established by Pike and Fries, well-known American linguists, there are two bases for classification :inflectional and functional.

Inflectional or morphological classes are determined by suffixes a word can take. A word is a noun if it can take the plural morpheme. A word is a verb if it can /iŋ/ or the past morpheme. A word is an

adjective if it can take /-ar/ or/ ɨst/ .

On the other hand, functional or syntactic classes are determined by the function a word performs in a specific sentence. This function is con- trolled by the position or slot that word fills. This means that the inflect- tional class of a certain word is static whereas its functional class is dynamic, i.e., changeable according to its position un different sentences.

For example, a nominal is what fills the slot in *his*———— . A verbal is whatever fills the slot in *He can*————an adjectival is whatever fills the slot in *He is a* ————*boy*.

The teacher may benefit from the possible application of the tagme- mic theory. In fact, pattern practice, which will be illustrated later in this chapter, is based on these tagmemic slots and slot fillers.

Further, the teacher may use such formulas to test and teach the syn- tactic class of a word. However, there is some doubt if he can   benefit from inflectional classes as defined by tagmemists because such classification
is strongly criticized for several reasons. For example, *pretty* is an adjective because it takes /-ar/ and /ist/, but, according to tagmemics, *beautiful* is not an adjective because it cannot take the suffixes /-ar/ or /ist /.This shows how semantics is sacrificed by tagmemics for the sake of morphology, which makes morphological classification a bit artificial.

III. 2. 4. *Transformational Grammar* :

Transformational grammar is a modern linguistic theory which appeared
in the 1950's and was established by an American linguist called Noam Chomsky and modified by several other linguists later.

This theory represent a reaction to all previous grammar theories.
Such a reaction manifests itself in many ways :

1. According to transformational grammar every sentence has a deep structure and a surface structure.

2. The deep structure is turned into a surface one through optional
and obligatory transformational rules.

3. This grammar is characterized by explicitness, which means that
the grammar accounts for all linguistic facts explicitly without leaving
some facts to the reader's intelligence.

4. This grammar is supposed to be formal, i.e., symbolized and quasi mathematical because it uses symbols, abbreviations, formula-like descrip- tions, numbers, and the like.

The teacher who is familiar with such grammar can make use of it in teaching foreign languages. Personal experiences has shown that students
find great interest in formalized transformational rules provided that such
rules that given in the right way and doses that suit the learners' level.
Such rules have proved to be quite effective in teaching some grammar relations such as active-passive , statement-interrogation, affirmative-nega- tive, simple-compound, and simple-complex structures.

III. 3. *Grammatical Meaning* :

The meaning of a sentence is derived from two sources : its lexemes, i.e., words, and its grammar. Lexemes supply us with a part of meaning called the lexical meaning. On the other hand, the grammar build-up of a certain sentence supplies us with another part of meaning called the gram- matical meaning.

The grammatical meaning consist of four components : syntax, function words, intonation, and inflections. These components will be discussed briefly in the following sections.

III. 3. 1. Syntax :

The sentence syntax is one determinant of grammatical meaning. Syn- tax refers to the order of words within the same sentence. To get a clear idea of how syntax controls meaning, let us examine these four sentences :

1. The men killed and lion and the tiger.

2. The tiger killed the men and the lion.

3. The lion killed the men and the tiger.

4. The tiger and the lion killed the men.

In each of above sentences, the lexical units are identical : men, tiger, lion, killed, and the. Nevertheless, each sentence has a different meaning. The reason for these differences in meaning among the four sen- tences is the difference in the intra-sentence order of words.

The teacher has to be conscious of the syntactic variable as a deter- minant of meaning. Further, he should pass this consciousness to his students through appropriate explanations and drills.

III. 3. 2. Function Words :

Words may be classified into two types : content words and function words . Content words constitute the main body of words in a language. Such type of words includes nouns, pronouns, adjectives, verbs, and adverbs.

On the other hand, function words are a closed class of words. The number of such words in English is about two hundred out of the half mil- lion words of that language. Function words include auxiliaries, preposi- tions, conjunctions, relatives, interrogatives, articles, and adverbs of degree.

Concerning meaning, content words express the major part of it whereas function words add to it some clarifications and relations that are essential. In the sentence, *the boy will go to the school, the* marks nominality and denotes definition: will marks verbality and denotes futurity: *to* marks nominality and denotes direction. However, if the sentence is made to contain content words only, one can still understand the greater part of its message through the hypothetical sentence of *boy go school.*

In teaching, function words are to be taught as parts of grammatical structures. This means that the method of teaching function words is quite different from that of teaching content words. While teaching function words, we emphasize a certain pattern, whereas while teaching content words, we emphasize the words themselves, which may be used in a variety of patterns.

To put it differently, when we teach a grammatical structure, we keep the pattern constant and vary words in drilling that structure. In contrast, when we teach a content word, e keep that word consonant and vary pat- terns in drilling that word.

III. 3. 3. Intonation :

The third determinant of grammatical meaning is intonation. Two sen- tences may have the same content and function words concatenated in the same order, but they still differ in meaning owing to a difference in intona- tion. For verification, let us examine these two sentences :

1. ^{2}You wrote two letters ^{3}ysterday^{1} ↘.

2. 2You wrote two letters ^{3}yesterday^{3} ↗ ?

The first sentence has the /231 ↘ / intonation pattern which marks a statement if the sentence does not start with a wh-word. The second sen- tence has the /233 ↗ / intonation pattern, which marks a yes-no interroga- tion, i.e., a question beginning with an auxiliary and requiring a response that starts with yes or no. this statement-question contrast has solely originated from difference in intonation, which proves that intonation is one determinant of grammatical meaning.

The pedagogical implication of this fact is that the teacher has to teach the intonation of the grammatical patterns as an inseparable part of it since changing intonation normally causes a change in meaning.

III. 3. 4. Inflection :

The fourth determinant of grammatical meaning is inflections or
inflectional morphemes. Such morphemes are suffixes added to words
with some effect on meaning but without affecting the class of the stem.
For example, /s/ in *books* is an inflection that added some meaning to *book* but both *book* and
books are nouns.

These inflectional morphemes are limited in number:

1. The plural morpheme. It has several varieties, among which are /s/, /z/, and /tz/, which are
phonetically conditioned as was explained in the previous chapter. This morpheme is added to
nouns to mean plurality, i.e., more than one in English.

2. The possessive morpheme. It has several varieties, three of
which are identical with the varieties of the plural morpheme, e.g., *the men's car*, *Robert's book*,
and *John's house*. This morpheme means belongingness or possession and is added to a noun.

3. The progressive morpheme, /iŋ/.it is added to verbs to mean continuity.

4. The present morpheme. It has three varieties of /s/,/z/. and / ɨz/ and is added to the verb
in the present simple tense when the subject is a third person singular.

5. The past morpheme. It has several allomorphs, among which are /t/, /d/, and / ɨd/. It is
added to the verb to mean the past tense.

6. The past participle morpheme. It is added to the verb to mean passivity or the aspect of
perfection.

7. The comparative morpheme, /ar/. It is added to the adjective to mean *more*.

8. The superlatives morpheme, / ɨst/. It is suffixed to the adjective
to mean *most*.

These inflectional suffixes contrast with another type of suffixes
called derivational suffixes in several ways :

1. Inflectional suffixes do not usually affect the class of a word : a noun remains a noun, a
verb remains a verb, and so on. On the other hand, derivational suffixes may change the word
class, e.g., *move*(ment), *teach*(er).

politic(al). However, a derivational suffix may not affect the class, e.g., *psycholog(ist)*, *history(ian)*.

2. As for number, inflectional suffixes are few, whereas derivational ones are numerous.

3. As for sequence and position, inflectional suffixes close the
word, which means that no other suffixes, whether derivational or inflect- tional, can come after the inflectional suffix. On the other hand, derivational suffixes allow other derivational and inflectional suffixes to follow
them. However, derivational suffixes have to occur in a special sequence within the same word.

The teacher is expected to make his students conscious of these inflectional morphemes because these morphemes are of high frequency,
mark word classes, and add to the lexical meaning of the word other semantic and grammatical dimensions such as plurality, continuity, pos- session, comparativeness, and tense.

III. 4. Sentence and Pattern :

The two concepts of pattern and sentence have sometimes been con- fused. Of course, the two terms are related but one is not the other. The pattern, to begin with, is the design underlying the sentence. To make the two concepts clearer , let us draw this comparison between them :

1. The sentence is the actual utterance, whereas the pattern is some- how like the formula of that sentence.

2. The sentences of a language are infinite in number, but its patterns are quite limited.

3. Each sentence corresponds to one pattern, but each pattern cor- responds to a countless number of sentences.

Nevertheless, linguists of English have shown a great deal of disagree ment on how many patterns their language has. The number of patterns they have offered ranges between six and sixteen. If the minimal number is to be taken, the major patterns of English will be the following :

1. Noun   + Verb + Adjective
2. Noun   + Verb
3. Noun   + Verb + Noun

4. Noun + Verb + Adverb

5. Noun + Verb + Noun + Noun

6. There + be + Noun + Adverb

These patterns may be exemplified by the following sentences res- pectively :

1. He + is + active.

2. He + has come.

3. John + did +it.

4. They + ran + quickly.

5. She + sent + him + a letter.

6. There + is + a book + on the table.

The previous sentences are considered to be condensed examples of those patterns. Other sentence forms are just expansions of the major pat- terns. For example, the third pattern, Noun + verb + Noun, may be expanded into a sentence like this one : the hard-working student + has been reading + an interesting five-hundred-page novel since six o'clock. Although the pattern is basically three units, it has been expanded into a sentence of fifteen words and is liable to more expansion.

III. 5. Pattern Practice :

If patterns are the underlying designs of sentences and if a pattern can be expressed by numerous sentences, there has to be a kind of prac- tice that dwells on the pattern we want to teach and at the same time use different sentences that express the same pattern. This practice is called pattern practice, which is usually defined as repetition of the pattern with variation of words.

Further, pattern practice involves shifting the learner's attention from the focus to be learned to other areas. Such a shift is adopted to raise pro- duction to the level of automaticity since we aim at developing the ability of the leaner to produce sentences at a fairly normal speed. The nature of pattern practice is best understood through actual examples of substitution drills, which are presented in the following sections.

III. 5. 1. Substitution Drills :

Substitution drills are grammatical drills within the method of pattern practice. These drills vary in the position to be substituted, the number of cues, the nature of cues, and the effect of cues.

1. Substitution with a fixed position. In this type of drilling, the cues given by the teacher are to be placed in the same slot, e.g., the slot of the subject, verb, or object. If the key sentence is *John ate the apple*, the drill may go this way :

Teacher : Mary.

Student : Mary ate the apple.

Teacher : He.

Student : He ate the apple.

Teacher : Robert.

Student : Robert ate the apple.

2. Substitution with a variable position. Here the teacher's cues fit in different slots. If the key sentence is *He ran quickly*, the drill may look like this:

Teacher : walked

Student : He walked quickly.

Teacher : she

Student : She walked quickly.

Teacher : slowly

Student : She walked slowly.

In this example, the cue has varied in position. The first cue is a verb: the second is the subject: the third is the adverb. Of course, this drill is more difficult than fixed substitution because it requires a higher skill on the part of the student, who has to grasp the cue and decide which slot suits that cue.

3. Simple substitution or substitution with one cue. The teacher gives one cue only at a time. The previous example also exemplifies this type of substitution.

4. Multiple substitution. Here the teacher gives more than one cue as a stimulus. Suppose that the key sentence is *Ali writes a letter every day*: the drill may proceed this way :

Teacher : Richard, week

Student : Richard writes a letter every week.

Teacher : Dick, month

Student : Dick writes a letter every month.

Teacher : receives, ten days

Student : Dick receives a letter every ten days.

It is obvious that multiple substitution is less easy for students than simple substitution because more cues are involved. Therefore, a teacher should start with simple drills and then proceed to multiple ones.

5. Substitution with oral cues. The teacher gives the cue orally: he pronounces the word.

6. Substitution with pictured cues. Here the teacher does not pro- nonce the cue; he shows the respondent a picture and the student places the corresponding word in the proper slot.

7. Substitution with concrete cues. Here the teacher uses no words or pictures; he shows the student the thing itself and the student is to sup- ply the word for the thing and places that word in the sentence.

It is clear that pictured cues or concrete cues are more difficult than oral cues. This is because the student has to do two things when a pictured or concert cue is presented : he has to recall the word and do the subs- titution. On the other hand, when an oral cue is provided, the student does the substitution only.

8. Substitution with a cue that causes no change. Here the cue just replace the original word without causing any changes in other words in the sentence. Suppose that the key sentence is *They studied hard last week*; the drill may go this way :

Teacher : We

Student : We studied hard last week.

Teacher : She

Student : She studied hard last week.

Teacher : I

Student : I studied hard last week.

9. Substitution with a cue that causes a change. Here the cue affects other words in the sentence. This normally happens when two words or
more have to be in concord or agreement in the same sentence such as
the subject and its verb, the noun and its pronoun, and the verb and its adverb of time. Suppose that the key sentence is *He came yesterday*; the drill may be :

Teacher : Now
Student : He is coming now.
Teacher : Tomorrow
Student : He will come tomorrow.
Teacher : Last week
Student : He came last week.

It goes without saying that a cue causing a change in other words is
more difficult than a cue that causes no change because the former re- quires knowledge of syntactic relationships between the component of
the same sentence. Therefore, cues causing a change are to be supplied
at a later stage.

10. Progressive substitution. In this drill, the key sentence gives
place to the sentence resulting from substitutions. In other words, when
a cue is given, it takes its position in the sentence of the previous res- ponse. Suppose that the key sentence is *John is a good friend*; the drill will go progressively this way :

Teacher : George

Student : George is a good friend.

Teacher : doctor

Student : George is a good doctor.

Teacher : hard-working

Student : George is a hard-working doctor.

11. Non-progressive substitution. This type of drill contrasts with

the pervious one. In the non-progressive substitution all cues are placed in the initial sentence, i.e., the key sentence. Let us use the same key sen- tences and the same cues as used in progressive substitution in order to get a clear idea about how the two drills differ.

Teacher : George

Student : George is a good friend.

Teacher : doctor

Student : John is a good doctor.

Teacher : hard-working

Student : John is a hard-working friend.

III. 5. 2. Loop Drill :

This is another type of substitution drills, where cues keep on chang- ing the sentence until the drills ends with the same sentence it started
with. If the key sentence is I saw *Ali crossing the street*, the drill may go on like this :

Teacher : Ahmad

Student : I saw Ahmad crossing the street.

Teacher : river

Student : I saw Ahmad crossing the river.

Teacher : Ali

Student : I saw Ali crossing the river.
Teacher : street
Student : I saw Ali crossing the street.

As one can easily notice, the final sentence in the drill is identical
with the key sentence. Of course, the cues in the classroom situation may
be equal in number to the number of students in a certain class. But here, in this example, the cues are limited in number because the purpose is
just to exemplify the drill.

III. 5. 3. Chain Drill :

This is usually a non-substitutional drill. After the teacher teaches the

form and meaning of a certain pattern, he gives the class the opportunity
to practice it. One way of conducting this practice is to let Student 1 ask
a certain question. Student 2 will answer and ask the same question to Stu-dent 3, who will answer and then ask student 4.this procedure continues
until all students have the chance to ask and answer in a chain-like man- ner, where each ring is linked to the one before it and to the one after it. The advantage of such a drill is to train students not only to respond to questions but to form questions as well. Further, such a drill creates a spe- cial social atmosphere in the classroom, where students are not only asked by the teacher but by their classroom also, which may be a fairly
new experience to most students.

To give an example of chain drills, let us consider these stimuli and responses :

Student 1 : What is your name ?

Student 2 : My name is Zaki.
    What is your name ?

Student 3 : My name is Fuad.
    What is your name ?

Student 4 : My name is Basheer.
    What is your name ?

III. 5. 4. Four-phased Drill :

As the name of this drill indicates, the drill consists of four phases in the following order:

1. The teacher gives the stimulus, which may be a cue for substitu- tion or a question.

2. A student responds to the teacher's stimulus.

3. The teacher repeats the correct response.

4. The whole class repeats after the teacher.

Let us consider these sentences as an example of four-phased drills :
Teacher : When does the lesson start ?
Student : It starts at eight o'clock.

Teacher : It starts at eight o'clock.

Class : It starts at eight o'clock.

A four-phased drill is usually effective for more than one reason:
1. It gives room for individual practice through the second phase.

2. It gives room for listening to the teacher's model answer and mo- del pronunciation through the third phase.

3. It gives room for everybody in the class to participate through choral repetition in the fourth phase.

III. 6. Grammar Exercises :

The previously mentioned drills are basically oral ones. However, some of them may be employed for writing purposes. This section will pre- sent some types of grammar exercise that are basically reading exer- cises, i.e., seen exercises. However, some of these exercises, if not all, may be used orally, depending on the class level and the students' ability to recall long stimuli. Here are some of these grammar exercises :

1. Integration or synthesis. Two sentences or more are synthesized into one by means of conjunctions or relatives. The output may be a com- pound sentence or complex one. The exercise may supply the connector or require the student to provide the suitable one, e.g., he passed *the test + he did not study* $\longrightarrow$ although he did not study, he passed the test.

2. Addition. One word or more are given and are to be placed in the proper position in a grammatically complete sentence, e.g., *he comes early*(often)$\longrightarrow$ he often comes early. This exercise develops *the students consciousness of syntax*, i.e., word order within a sentence.

3. Completion. One clause of a complex sentence is given, whether the main cause or the subordinate one, and the missing clause is to be supplied, e.g., *if you ask him,-*. Such an exercise involves the production of a grammatical structure, thinking of a semantically and logically conve- nient completion, and providing for the sequence of tenses and adverbs in the two clauses of the same sentence.

4. Contraction or abbreviation.The full form is to be changed into the short one, e.g., he will be back soon $\longrightarrow$ he'll be back soon.

5. Transformation. A sentence is transformed into another, e.g., the active voice into the passive voice, a direct speech into an indirect

one, a sentence with singulars into one with plurals, and a statement into a question.

6. Expansion. Optionally deleted words are re-supplied in a sentence, e.g., *the man (running there) is his father* → *the man (who is run- ning there) is his father.*

7. Replacement. A word is to replace a phrase and to do the same syntactic function, e.g., *he went (to the town)* → *he went (there).*

8. Filling-in. a missing word has to be supplied in a sentence , e.g., *the letter...written yesterday* → *the letter (was) written yesterday.*

9. Word ordering. The student is required to re-arrange a group of words to form a useful sentence, e.g., *found, he, has, his, book* → *he has found his book.*

10. Maximal deletion. A sentence is to be reduced to its minimal components through maximum deletion, e.g., *the ripe, red apple was eaten by John* → *the apple was eaten.*

11. Pronominalization. Some or all nouns in a sentence are to be changed into pronouns.

12. Multiple choice. Several answers are given and the student is to select the only answer that is right. Such an exercise is of a recognition nature since the student does not produce anything of his own; he just recognizes the right answer among a list of other answers.

13. Form modification. A word is to be modified so as to suit the sentence context, e.g., *he (not finish) yet* → *he has not finished yet.*

14. Parallel structure. A group of words is given so as to form a sentence grammatically parallel to a provided model sentence, e.g., *tea, hot, drink* → *the tea is too hot to drink.*

As was previously mentioned, these exercises are basically seen and written exercises. Nevertheless, they may be used as oral drills, but this depends on the pattern difficulty, the sentence length, and class level.

III. 7. Situational Grammar :

Situational grammar implies that a grammatical structure is accom- panied by a real situation provided by the teacher or students especially

when a new structure is handled. Such situationalization has proved to be quite effective because it makes grammatical structures highly meaningful, helps to clarify the meaning of the pattern, and adds liveliness to the lesson.

The teacher can achieve this situationalized grammar through several ways :

1. Actual examples. Instead of using imaginary sentences, the
teacher is advised to use real examples related to himself, his students,
their school and their actual life and experiences.

2. Real names. The teacher is advised to use the names of his students in his sentences and attach to those names actual actins, habits, and facts.

3. Verifiable sentences. If general sentences are to be needed, it
is better to choose those verifiable ones, i.e., true ones. This means that
the sentence has to be in accordance with general facts of life and
science.

4. Action. The teacher can use actions to teach some structures
at least. This works best in the case of teaching verbs that denote actions. i.e., dynamic verbs. For example, he may say," I am going to clean the black- board.". then while he is cleaning it, he says," I am cleaning it." After he finishes his cleaning, he says, " I have cleaned it."

5. Dramatization. The teacher may introduce some purposive dia- logues to reinforce some structures and ask his students to memorizes such dialogues and recite them at class.

It is noteworthy that situational grammar is not an alternative to
pattern practice but, on the contrary, it has to supplement it. The former emphasizes the meaning of a pattern, whereas the latter emphasizes its
form. In fact, pattern practice is criticized by some methodologists for neg- lecting meaning for the sake of form, fluency, and automaticity, which
may be unfortunately true. Consequently, there is a need to use both pat- tern practice and situationalization and let them complete one another
instead of competing with one another.

111. 8. Visual Grammar :

It is also advisable that the teacher visualizes grammatical facts and relationships. Such visualization may take the form of diagrams drawn on charts or the chalkboard to summarize, contrast, or synthesize patterns already learned by students. In addition, demonstrating examples on some grammatical patterns by writing them on the chalkboard is another way of visualization, which is certainly an aid to learning.

Visualization facilitates learning a new material or reviewing an old material by passing the learning material through the eye gate. As a result, this visual perception will reinforce the previous aural perception. For example, in teaching tenses, a line representing time may be drawn and divided into three units of past, present, and future extensions; each exten- sion is then divided into three units of simple, perfect and continuous aspects. Similarly, in teaching or reviewing repositions, a circle may be drawn and prepositions may be placed outside, on, and, inside the circle to show visually how prepositions contrast with each other.

III. 9. General Remarks :

While teaching grammatical structures, it is recommended to remem- ber these remarks :

1. Generalizations, which are often called rules, are helpful to both teachers and students provided they are given in the proper time and manner. These generalizations summarize the behavior of language and help students to control their usage of the foreign language.

2. Concepts such as subject and object may be given in the second- dary stage, but not to beginners. These concepts are in fact needed in phrasing generalizations.

3. Comparing related patterns strengthens learning because it helps the learner see where those patterns are similar and where they are dif- ferent.

4. The meaning of a pattern is not to be sacrificed for the sake of its form.

5. Written exercises should play their role in reinforcing oral drills on grammatical patterns.

6. The variation of teaching methods and techniques is necessary for maintaining students' attention and motivation and for attacking the learning target from all possible sides.

7. Continual reviewing is essential for optimal and permanent learning. It is also essential for working against the inevitable effect of time, i.e., forgetting.

8. In large classes, choral repetition may replace group and individual repetition for obvious practical reasons. In small classes, chorus repetition is followed by group repetition, which is followed by individual repetition.

9. While teaching patterns, vocabulary has to be controlled or kept easy. When the teacher is presenting new patterns, he has to use familiar words. Similarly, when he is presenting new words, he has to use familiar patterns. The underlying principle is to teach one new thing at a time so as to control the difficulty level of the taught material.

III. 10. *Presentation* :

When teaching a new pattern, one may follow these steps :

1. Example. Write on the chalkboard an example of the pattern you want to teach.

2. Focus. Draw the learners' attention to the specific structure you want them to learn by underlining that structure or by using colored chalk.

3. Meaning. Present the meaning of the structure preferably through a situation, action, dramatization, or a context. However, the native langu- age may be used, if necessary, to present meaning or to check understand- ing of the presented meaning.

4. Form. After the presentation of meaning, disuses with your class the form of that pattern. Form may involve factors such as concord, order of words, inversion, inflections, or some function words.

5. Contrast. Explain or discuss with your class how this new pattern is different from or similar to another related pattern or patterns already learned. Such a comparison may handle both areas of meaning and form.

6. Reinforcement. Give more examples to reinforce their compre- hension of both meaning and form.

7. Parallel examples. Let your students give parallel structures, i.e., examples similar to the new pattern in form. You may ask them questions that lead to those parallel sentences.

8. Generalization. Help your class derive any possible generalize-
tions especially regarding the pattern form. You may ask them to take note
of those generalizations.

9. Oral drills. Start some suitable oral drills on the new pattern
such as substitution drills with their various types, chain drills, loop drills,
and four-phased drills. Here the teacher's cures and student's responses
are conducted orally.

10. Visual exercises. The textbook usually contains at least one exercise on each new pattern.
Let students do the related exercise orally. In contrast with oral drills, in the visual exercise, the
stimulus is given by the textbook but the response is oral.

11. Written exercises. After doing the textbook exercise orally, let
the class write down the exercise in their exercise books. Such writing process is an additional
source of reinforcement to learning obtained
through aural, oral, and visual media.

III. 11. Discussion :

1. How can we benefit from each grammar theory in teaching pat- terns ?

2. What are the advantages and limitations of pattern practice ?

3. Make a drill of your own to exemplify each type of substation
drills. Let each drill contain at least ten cues with their responses.

4. Give an example of your own on each of the following : loop, chain, and four-phased
drills. Each drill is to consist of at least ten stimuli with their responses.

5. Give five exemplary sentences on each type of grammar exercise.

6. Choose any grammatical structure and show how you may teach
it to a specified level of students.

TEACHING VOCABULARY

This chapter will deal with vocabulary, its types, meaning, word from, selection of vocabulary, knowing a word, and the step of teaching vocabulary.

IV. 1. A Word :

A word may be defined as the minimal free meaningful unit. This definition makes a word different from a morpheme, which is the smallest meaningful unit . This implies that a word may consist of one morpheme or more. For example, *boy* is one word consisting of one morpheme whereas *boys* is one word consisting of two morphemes, i.e., the *boy* morpheme and the plurality morpheme.

Further, a word consist of a radical element, called a root, to which some prefixes, suffixes, or infixes may be added. Once an affix or more are added to the root, the outcome may be a stem or base to which other affixes are added. For example, in the word *civilization*, *civil* is the root, *ize* and *tion* are suffixes, but civilize is the stem or base.

Each morpheme in the word is either bound or free. A bound morpheme, which may be a root or an affix, cannot stand alone as an independent word. On the other hand, a free morpheme can stand alone as an independent word. For example, *playing* is a word consisting of a free root and a bound suffix.

In addition, each word has a meaning, a form, and a distribution. Each

word is either content word or a function word. Each word is either active
or passive at a certain level. Details come in the following sections.

Sometimes words are referred to as lexical units, lexemes or vocabu- lary items. The total vocabulary of a certain language is sometimes called
the lexicon of that language.

IV. 2. Passive and Active Vocabulary :

In teaching vocabulary, one has to distinguish two types of vocabulary : the passive and the active. Passive vocabulary is taught to be merely recognized and understood by the student upon hearing or reading that
kind of vocabulary. In contrast, active vocabulary is taught to be produced
by the student whenever it is needed in speaking or writing. To con-
clued, passive vocabulary is learned for recognition, but active vocabulary
is learned for production.

As for the teacher, he has to emphasize active vocabulary more than passive vocabulary. While dealing with the former type, the teacher has to focus on the meaning, pronunciation, spelling, and usage of involved words. While dealing with passive vocabulary, it suffices to teach the meaning
only since the objective of teaching here is more recognition.

In comparing passive vocabulary to active vocabulary, one may notice the following points:

1. Words passive at a certain level may become active at another level. In fact, learning involves the movement of some passive words from
the outer circle of recognition to the inner circle of active production.
With more learning, some words that were passively learned may become actively learned later.

2. Words passive for a certain purpose in a certain situation may be active for another purpose and another situation. This shows speculation as
a factor in word usage, each field of knowledge has its terms and technical vocabulary, which is certainly active for a specialist in a specific field but may not be so a specialist in other fields.

3. Passive vocabulary is usually larger in number than active vocabulary, a fact that applies to all persons speaking a native language or a foreign one. This implies that a person usually understands many more words than he actually uses.

4. Passive vocabulary is needed in listening or reading because what is required in these two skills is perception, whether aural or visual, followed by comprehension. On the other hand, active vocabulary is needed during speak- ing or writing because what is required in these two skills is thinking and expression.

5. One's active vocabulary in writing is usually larger than one's active vocabulary during speaking. One can easily notice that while writing one uses words one does not remember while speaking. One underlying reason may be the time factor: in writing, a person usually has more time to think and recall previously learned material and vocabulary. Another reason may be that we are usually more frequently evaluated for what we write than for what we say, which necessitates more carefulness in word selection. A third reason may be the nature of content: in writing, the topic is usually somehow technical and more formal than the topic in speaking. As a result, writing vocabulary tends to be more specialized and in a way wider than speaking vocabulary.

IV. 3. Function and Content Words :

In the previous section, vocabulary has been classified into active and passive types. In this section, vocabulary is classified into two other types from a different point of view: function words and content words.

Function words are sometimes called grammatical words. They are also referred to as empty words or structural words. These different names for the same thing may tell something about the nature of such words :

1. They are called grammatical words because they have a special grammatical function.

2. They are empty words because they do not have much meaning if compared to content words.

3. Function words are limited in number about two hundred words in English. This list includes auxiliaries, prepositions, conjunctions, rela- tives, interrogatives, articles, and adverbs of degree. In comparison, content words are the rest of the English vocabulary, which is approximately half a million words.

4. Function words are essential for establishing the grammaticality of sentences, but content words are essential for providing sentences with

their basic message. For example, if e say, *boy go school*, most of the message is conveyed to the listener. However, when we say, *The boy has gone to school*, the whole message is conveyed and the sentence is brought to grammaticality.

The pedagogical implication of this classification is that function words are to be taught as a part of grammar and, consequently, taught in patterns and in the same methods as used in teaching grammatical structures. On the other hand, content words are taught as words. i.e., in the methods designed for teaching words, and not as structures.

IV. 4. Word Meaning :

The branch of linguistics that deals with meaning is called semantics.
In this branch, there are certain principles to be remembered :

1. The meaning of a word may change through time but this temporal factor works slowly : it may take several scores of years, if not centuries,
to have such semantic change. It is obvious that words do not change
their meaning every week or every year.

2. The meaning of a word may differ from one dialect to another. Such differences may be consciously or unconsciously exercised by the speakers of a certain dialect to make themselves somehow distinguishable from other communities.

3. The word is not the thing because the word is just a symbol arbitrarily associated with its referent.

4. A word may have more than one meaning. An easy and quick veri- fication of this is just to have a look at a dictionary, where one can rarely find a word that has one meaning only.

5. The meaning of a word may change from one context to another.

For a teacher, these principles should have their implication. In teach- ing, it is better to present a word in a certain context, because in another context the word may have a different meaning. Similarly, in testing, it
sounds unwise to ask about the meaning of isolated words because, in isolation, a word may mean different things.

IV. 4. 1. Types of Meaning :

Semantic meaning may be denotative or connotative. Every content

63

word has a denotation, but only some content words have connotative meanings.

The denotative meaning of a word is an objective meaning, which does not differ from one person to another. It is a colorless meaning, because it is devoid of any personal or emotional experiences. In other words, it is the dictionary meaning of the word and thus it is the meaning common to all speakers of a certain language.

In contrast, the connotative meaning of a word is a subjective meaning, which differs from one individual to another. It is a colored meaning, because it carries personal and emotional experiences.

For example, the denotation of "cow" is that animal we all know or, as one dictionary puts it, a domestic, female, bovine animal. But the connotation of the word "cow" may differ from one country to another or from one person to another: to a Buddhist, a cow is a symbol of holiness: to a poor farmer, it is a food securer: to a child once kicked by a cow, it is a rather terrible creature.

In teaching words, what often matters most is the denotation of the word, because it is a universal and objective meaning. However, since emotion is an actual part of life and since personal experience is also an actual reality, there is room for touching upon word connotations especially when those connotations are strongly associated with their words such as *father, mother, home, religion, God, son,* and many others.

IV. 4. 2. Presentation of Meaning :

The meaning of a new word may be presented in several ways :

1. Direct association. The new word is taught by the direct associa- tion of the word and its referent. This method is best applicable in the case of words referring to concrete thing existent in the classroom itself such
as *desk, table, ceiling, floor,* and *chalkboard.*

2. Picture. If the referent itself cannot be brought to the class-
room, its picture, whether a photograph or a drawing, can be used to teach the meaning of a certain word.

3. Action. The meaning of some words may be presented through acting. This method works best in teaching the meaning of verbs such as *run, walk, move, laugh, smile,* and *speak.*

4. Context. A word may be used in sentence or a group of sentences which lead to the students' understanding of meaning.

5. Synonym. The meaning of a new word may be taught by giving a synonymous word i.e., a word semantically equivalent. Of course, the given synonym has to be familiar to students: otherwise, it will be an added problem and will be of no help in explaining the meaning of the new word.

6. Antonym. The meaning of a word may be explained through an antonym, i.e., a word semantically opposite. Similar to the synonym, the antonym has to be a familiar word as well.

7. Definition. The meaning of some words may be presented through definition, which can be stated by limiting the class function, location, or qualities of a certain referent.

8. Translation. If the referent is an abstract one, the native language equivalent of that word may be used. Further, such an equivalent may be given if other techniques prove to be imoractical or ineffective with some words. The teacher, through experience, will gain more knowledge in
choosing the proper techniques that suits a specific word.

IV. 5. Word Form :

Each word has two forms of expression : [1] the oral form, *i.e.*, the pronunciation of the word and [2] the written or graphic form, *i.e.*, its spelling. When a new word is taught, we have to teach these two forms especially in the case of active vocabulary.

Concerning the internal structure of the word form, each word has a root or a base, which may be joined to other morphemes called affixes. These affixes are of three types :

1. Prefix. It is an affix fixed before the root, e.g., (en) courage,(in)credi- ble, (dis)believe.

2. Infix. It is an affix fixed inside the root, e.g.,f(ee)t,r(a)n, s(u)ng.

3. Suffix. It is an affix fixed at the end of the root, e.g., probabil(ity), rich(ness), wid(en).

Since these affixes recur very frequently, it will be quite useful and economical if the teacher gives his students the meanings of these

65

affixes and calls their attention to their spelling. Of course, this affix orientation has to be done with the proper level of students and in slight doses. Such orientation may help in several ways:

1. Students will easily understand the meaning of a new word if the root is familiar to them. A student who knows the meaning of the suffixes *en*, *-ness*, and *–ly* and the root 'wide' will not find it difficult to grasp the meaning of the words 'widen', 'wideness' and 'widely' even when he comes across such words for the first time.

2. If affixes are focused on with respect to their spelling, mistakes in spelling affixes will be reduced to the minimum. If students learn that the suffix *–ess* is written with double *s*, students invariably write it so wherever it occurs. This will decrease the learning lead and minimize spelling errors especially in writing affixes.

3. Learning affixes will also help students to derive new words from already known words.

IV. 6. *Vocabulary Counts* :

Several linguists have designed some lists of vocabulary items. They believed such lists would be adequate for communication .The motive of those linguists is to make learning English as a foreign language as easy as possible. As a result, they selected from the 500,000 words of English a limited number of words which can perform the main function of language, i.e., communication.

The following are examples of those lists:

1. Basic English. It is a list of 850 words, eighteen of which are verbs. This list was described by Winston Churchill as suitable to be an international language.

2. General Service List. It is a list of 2,000 words designed by Michael West.

3. Thorndike's Lists. This specialist made three lists of ten thousand, twenty thousand, and thirty thousand words respectively.

All those lists have shown a great deal of agreement on the first five hundred words. This differences among these lists may be attributed to differences in the goals of these word counts. If the goals of teaching English include the ability to read English books, for example, the words of Basic English are certainly inadequate for such an objective. Another reason for list differences may be the nature of counted materials, whether written or spoken. These materials were used to count the frequency of occurrence of involved words. Of course, conclusions on the most frequent words depend on the nature and content of the counted corpus. If corpora are different, conclusions will inevitably be different and this is what has hap- pened with specialists working on word counts.

However, it is held that the minimum number of words adequate for reading English books is seven thousand words. It is also held that the minimum number of words adequate for writing in English is three thousand.

IV. 7. Difficulty Levels :

Not all words are of equal difficulty. The difficulty level depends on several variables :

1.   Number of syllables. Holding other things consonant, a long word, i.e., with more syllables, letters, or phonemes, has a higher probability of causing some difficulties in spelling or pronunciation than a short word.

2.   Concrete versus abstract. A word referring to a concrete being tends to be more easily taught and grasped than a word referring to an abstract concept.

3.   Graphic-phonemic correspondence. A word that shows correspond dence between its graphemes and its phonemes is easier to spell and pronounce than a word that lacks such correspondence. For example, words such as net, fit, kid, swim, and bed have a one-to-one correspondence between their graphic transcription and their phonemic transcription. In other words, they are written the way they are spoken, which makes them easy to spell and read.

4.   Problem phonemes. If all the phonemes of a word in the foreign language do exist in the native language, there will be no problems regar- ing the pronunciation of this word. On the other hand, if a word in the foreign language contains a phoneme or more that do not exist in the native language, that word may be difficult to pronounce and more practice is required in such cases.

5.   Form and meaning. It sometimes happens that a word in the foreign language has an equivalent in the native language similar in form, meaning, or both. For example, the English word 'cinema' has an equivalent

in Arabic of the same pronunciations and meaning. Further, Arabic words borrowed from English such as radio, telephone, and television are identical with their origins in meaning and similar in pronunciation. To conclude
more similarity between the words of the foreign language and the native language entails more easiness in teaching and learning those similar
words.

Educationally speaking, it is a well-established principle that the easy material is to be taught before the difficult material and the concrete before the abstract. This psycho-educational principle has to be abided by in teaching words of the target language. Fortunately, the gradation implied in this prince- ple is usually secured by the curriculum designer and the textbook author.

IV. 8. Vocabulary Selection :

What words are we to select from the big mass of target vocabulary ? After selection, the question remains : which words are we to teach first ? The answer to these two questions largely depends on the criteria for selection and priority. Different methodologists have employed different criteria such as :

1. Immediacy. Some educationists hold that it is better to start with words related to the learners' immediate environment, i.e., those concrete things around them.

2. Regularity. Some others believe we should first teach words that
are regular in their spelling, plurality, past ,and past participle. It is argued that such words make a good start because they are easier than irregular words.

3. Utility. Some believe we are to begin with useful words regardless of the degree of their immediacy or regularity.

4. Frequency. According to the frequency criterion, if a word is
highly frequent, it has to receive priority over less frequent words. If a
word is a technical one, it has to wait until later stages.

One may notice that these four criteria sometimes contradict one
another. For example, the criterion of regularity may oppose the criterion
of utility : a regular word may not be utilitarian and vice versa. Similarly, immediacy may contradict regularity.

However, there are cases where these criteria do overlap. For example, a frequent word is usually a useful one. Further, an immediate word is usually both useful and frequent. This indicates that the criteria of immediacy, utility, and frequency overlap with one another although they may contradict the criterion of regularity.

IV. 9. Knowing a Word :

If we want the learner to learn a word well, we have to teach it well since optimal learning is facilitated by effective teaching. This requires some kind of analysis of the components of word knowledge. Knowing a word fully means the following :

1. The leaner should be able to understand the meaning of that word upon hearing or reading it.

2. He should be able to spell it correctly when he needs it in writing.

3. He should be able to pronounce it correctly when he uses it in speaking.

4. He should be able to use that word correctly in a spoken or written sentence.

5. He should be able to read it correctly.

6. He should be able to do all the above ay a normal speed and without hesitation.

To put it differently, knowing a word means being able to say, under- stand, read, write, and use it correctly and at a fairly normal speed. Such indication of word knowing should be clear in the teacher's and the learner's mind because the teacher has to teach all those skills and the learner has to focus on them all as well.

IV. 10. Teaching Steps :

In teaching active vocabulary, one may follow these steps :

1. Students are to listen to the word first. In other words, the teacher pronounces the word two or three times with his students listening.

2. After listening to the teacher pronouncing the word, students repeat the word after the teacher.

3. The teacher helps students get the meaning of the word through any technique he finds suitable to that specific word.

4. The teacher uses the word in sentences to show the class how the word is actually used.

5. Students are asked to use the word in similar sentences. The teacher may ask students questions the answers of which require the usage of that word.

6. The teacher writes the word on the chalkboard and may draw his students' attention to any spelling problems related to that word.

7. Students read the word.

8. Students are asked to write down the words and their meanings in their notebooks.

IV. 11. *Discussion :*

1. Choose any one of your English textbooks and list twenty active words and twenty passive ones.

2. Make a list which contains thirty function words.

3. What is the difference between teaching function words and teach- ing content words ?

4. Choose any fifty English words and then grade them according to their difficulty levels starting with the easiest and including a justification for your gradation.

5. Evaluate the vocabulary items selected for any one the reading textbooks assigned to the intermediate stage here and set your evaluative criteria.

6. What modifications would you like to propose regarding the teaching steps mentioned in this chapter ?

TAECHING READING

Reading is one of the major skills involved in language reading. This chapter will deal with the various methods of teaching reading to beginners, reading objectives, reading types, the nature of the reading process, plan- ning a reading lesson, and some other related topics.

V. 1. Language Systems :

Languages differ in how writing represents speech. Concerning this representation, language may be categorized into three main systems :

1. The logographic system. According to this system, there is a different graphic symbol for each different word.

2. The syllabic system. In this system, there is a different graphic symbol or sign for each different syllable. An example of such a system
is Japanese.

3. The alphabetic system. In this system, there is a different graphic symbol, i.e., a letter or grapheme, for every phoneme or sound. Such a system is a development from the syllabic system, which is a development from the logographic system. This system, i.e., the alphabetic one, is the system followed by most modern languages nowadays. English and Arabic
are among those languages written alphabetically.

One way wonder why these writing systems are discussed in a chapter that deals with reading. The answer is obvious : the writing system is
itself a reading system because how we write determines how others will read.

V. 2. Methods of Teaching Reading :

There are four main methods for teaching reading to beginners. These methods may be used in teaching native languages or foreign languages.
The advantages or disadvantages of each method will be discusses in the following sections.

V. 2. 1. The Letter Method :

The stating point in letter method or the phonics method is to teach learners how to read the alphabet of the target or foreign language. After mastering the letters of the alphabet, learners are taught how to read words and then sentences.

V. 2. 2. The Global Method :

The global method resets on gestalt psychology, which assumes that we perceive wholes first rather than parts. According to this assumption, teaching the reading skill should start with sentences and then words. The last step is letter perception. In this sense, the global method goes in the opposite direc- tion of the letter method: the beginning point of one method is the ending point of the other.

The global method is sometimes referred to as the see-then-say me- thod. It is sometimes called the look-and-say method. These names some- how reflect the nature of the named method although all reading, no mat- ter which method is used, involves seeing and saying because nobody can read without seeing or feeling followed by saying. However, the implica- tion in these names is to look at the sentence or the word as a whole without cutting it into letters. In other words, the global method aims at developing the learner's ability to read globally, i.e., to read large units at a glance.

V. 2. 3. The Linguistic Method :

The linguistic method depends on some kind of linguistic analysis of the grapheme-phonemic relationships within the target language itself. In a language like English, the same grapheme may represent more than one phoneme. For example, the graphem t may stand for the phoneme/t/ or the phoneme /š/in the words 'table' and 'action' respectively. Similarly, the same phoneme may be represented by more than one grapheme. For example, the

72

phoneme /f/ may be graphically represented by *f, ph,* and *gh* in the words 'fine' photo' and 'enough' respectively. This indicates that the correspondence between phonemes and graphemes in English is not perfect.

However, there are some patterns that show a great deal of regu-larity controlling grapheme-phoneme relationships. These regular patterns according to the linguistic method, should be the starting point in teaching reading especially to beginners. In other words, reading has to be some- how programmed into what may be simply called reading patterns, which emphasize to the learner the regular relations between written forma and their pronunciation, i.e., between graphemes and their corresponding pho- nemes.

V. 2. 4. The Eclectic Method :

The eclectic method makes use of the previously mentioned three methods. The assumption underlying such eclecticism is that each method has something to offer for reading. The letter method is needed to develop letter consciousness, which is essential for both spelling and reading. The global method is needed to develop speed and resist some probable side effects of the letter method such as the tendency to continually split the word into letters. The linguistic method is needed to establish some reading pat- terns and thus minimizes pronunciation mistakes during reading.

V. 3. Reading Purposes :

It is important to get acquainted with the various purpose of reading because the reading purpose obviously influences the reading process in certain aspects. Different individuals may read for different purposes :

1. Reading for information. Some people may read aiming at gaining more general or specific knowledge.

2. Reading for research. Some people may read in order to review specializes literature related to a certain problem they intend to do research on.

3. Reading for summarizing. Some people may read a text to write a summary or a report on that text.

4. Reading for tests. Students often read in preparation for tests.

Some students, in fact, do not read their textbooks expect when a test is announced.

5. Reading for enjoyment. We sometimes read not to collect information, do research, summarize a text, or get ready for a test. We sometimes read for the sake of enjoyment. This may occur when we read a novel, a story, or a poem.

As was mentioned before, the reading purpose affects the reading pro- cess. When one reads to gather some data on a particular topic, one reads selectively. In other words, one focuses on related data and ignores material irrelevant to his objectives. Similarly, reading for research purposes proceeds selectively.

In contrast, reading a textbook for taking a test requires more con- centration on more details. The reader feels responsible for almost all
details and, not only that, but for implications as well. He is also obliged to read the material several times, it necessary, because he reads for recall,
not for mere data collection, which is usually recorded graphically with
less burden on memory.

On the other hand, reading for enjoyment is quite different from other types of reading. The former requires less concentration and re-reading
the text is often improbable in this case because recalling is not a main purpose here. Reading for enjoyment is free in motive and process : it is
the reader who determines what, why, and how to read simply because
he reads to enjoy and not to exhaust himself.

V. 4. Types of Reading :

Since there are different purposes for reading, it follows there are different types of reading, which will be discussed in the coming sections.

V. 4. 1. Intensive Reading :

The purpose of intensive reading is to teach new words and new pat- terns. Therefore, the reading material designed for intensive reading is
usually a little higher than the students' level.

In preparation for intensive reading, the teacher presents to the class unfamiliar words and unfamiliar patterns. After such presentation, the
reading material is discussed and handled thoroughly as to   content, spell- ing, grammar, vocabulary , and pronunciation.

V. 4. 2. Extensive Reading :

The reading material here is usually within or probably a little below the students' level. Its main purpose is enjoyment and reinforcement of previously learned vocabulary and grammatical structures. The reading material is usually a group of short stories or a novel. This type of read- ing is sometimes called supplementary reading because it is supposed to supplement intensive reading.

The teacher assigns a chapter for home reading. Students may be given questions on the assigned chapter to answer at home or may be required to prepare some questions with their answers depending on the class level. That chapter will be the subject of discussion in the follow ing period.

For the sake of clarification, one may draw this comparison between extensive reading and intensive reading :

1. Extensive material is usually read at home, whereas intensive material is usually read in class.

2. Concerning difficulty level, extensive material is normally within or a little below the students' abilities, but intensive material is normally above their abilities.

3. As to objective, extensive reading aims at reinforcing previous learning when intensive reading aims at teaching new items.

4. The nature of the reading material is different : extensive material is usually stories or novels but intensive material may be scientific, des- criptive, or argumentative as well.

5. Extensive material is covered at a speed higher than that of intensive material. In extensive reading, one may cover three to ten pages per period, whereas in intensive reading the maximum may not be more than a page. This speed difference may be attributed to the difference in the difficulty levels of reading texts.

6. Concerning duration, extensive reading takes a small part of the foreign language hours, about ten per cent. In contrast, intensive reading takes the lion's share from those hours, not less than fifty per cent.

7. As to function, extensive reading has a supplementary role in the foreign language program, but intensive reading plays an essential role.

In other words, extensive reading may be theoretically dispensed with without seriously damaging the program, whereas intensive reading may be considered as the main skeleton of the program.

V. 4. 3. Silent Reading :

Silent reading is reading for comprehension. It is described as silent because it is supposed to be performed silently, i.e., without labial move- ments or the vibration of vocal cords. This implies that graphic forms are visually perceived and then transformed into meanings and ideas without passing through the vocal stage.

Most of our reading, in fact, is done silently. A few people such as radio and television announcers find themselves obliged to read aloud. In consequence, silent reading is an important skill that has to be developed properly through guidance and practice.

In addition, the teacher is expected to help students develop their speed in silent reading. Such development involves increasing the learner's eye span, which is the quantity of words a reader's eye can catch from a written line at one glance. The larger the span is, the faster reading can go. One way to attain such increase in eye span is to make students read a certain passage under some pressure of time. This pressure forces the student to widen his eye span, decrease the number of regressive eye movements, and shorten the time between a span and another.

V. 4. 4. Oral Reading :

Reading aloud or oral reading is another type of reading that may be used in class on the condition that it is employed purposefully. Students may read aloud to give the teacher a chance their pronunciation, word stresses, pauses, intonation, and understanding.

Further, the teacher is advised to notice the following points in rela- tion to reading aloud :

1. Start with good students so that they may be good models for other classmates.

2. When you ask a student to read aloud, let him face the class. His facing the class draws the students' attention and creates some activity and change in the classroom situation. Moreover, facing people when reading or talking to them is the natural way of doing so.

3. Reading aloud is often criticized for the students' probable pas- sivity since only one student is taking part. To overcome such passivity, students are invited to correct mistakes made by the reader. Such invi-
tation usually urges most students to listen carefully and participate acti-
vely in the correction of mistakes.

4. Do not let one single student read for a rather long time so as to secure the participation of the maximal number of students. However,
this should not mean that a student is to read for a few seconds only. Let each student read a reasonable quantity of lines.

5. Do not carry on this activity of reading aloud for a long time in order to avoid probable boredom or sacrificing other language skills that
are more important than reading aloud.

6. Let reading aloud come after students' silent reading, class dis- cussion, and your model reading.

7. To make reading aloud more interesting, you may run a competi- tion among class groups to see which group reads best. Such competition
is usually highly motivating to learners : everybody wants his group to
win and listens most carefully to hunt other groups' mistakes.

V. 4. 5. Model Reading :

Model reading is reading performed by the teacher as an example to
be imitated by students when they read aloud. It usually comes after
silent reading and discussion but before students' reading aloud.

Model reading may take either of these two forms :
1. The teacher reads the whole passage with students listening to
him without repetition. This form may be called undivided model reading.

2. The second form is divided model reading. The teacher reads a sentence and students repeat that sentence after him. Then the teacher moves to the next sentences, with students repeating after each sentence.
If the sentence is rather long, the teacher has to divide it into meaningful units and pause after each unit so as to give students enough time to repeat.

The second form, i.e., divided model reading, has some advantages over the first form :

1. Divided model reading secures more participation on the stud-

ents' part because they read after their teacher instead of listening pas- sively in the case of undivided model reading.

2. Divided model reading makes students listen better to what the teacher says because they are required to imitate how the teacher reads.
On the other hand, in undivided model reading , students' attention is rela- tively less and students soon find themselves unable to follow.

3. In divided model reading, there are more chances for better imitation because students imitate immediately after each model sentence or unit. In contrast, in the case of undivided model reading, students have to wait until the teacher reads the whole passage before they start reading.

However, undivided model reading has its place. Reading the whole passage without intermediate interruptions of students' repetition may be
better for presenting enunciation, intonation, and the general sequence of ideas.

V. 4. 6. SQ3R :

SQ3R is the type of reading an advanced student to expected to often do in reading textbooks. SQ3R consists of these five steps :

1. Survey (S). The student starts with surveying the book or chap- ter he intends to read. This survey provides the reader with a general
idea about the content of the reading material : its sequence, assump-
tions, main themes, and conclusions.

2. Questions (Q). After surveying, the student sets some major questions the reading material aims at giving answers to. These questions guide the reader, in the following steps, to the information he has to focus on and the answers he has to look for.

3. Reading (R). After setting the main questions, the student reads
the text, preferably with a pen in his hand to underline key concepts and prominent ideas, add some comments or symbols of his own, and to num- ber some classifications.

4. Recitation (R) . Then the student recites what he has read in a process similar to self-testing or self-evaluation. Through this process,
the student will be able to check whether he can recall what he has read
or not.

5. Review (R). In light of recitation, the student can locate which parts the text he can recall and which parts he cannot recall. This location will guide him in his review, which is. Necessary for overcoming the effect of forgetting partly caused by the mere elapsing of time.

To conclude, SQ3R is the type of reading usually used with textbooks and it secures several conditions of good comprehension : comprehen- siveness through surveying, purpsiveness through questions, comprehension through the first reading, self-evaluation through recitation, and
re-learning through reviewing.

V. 4. 7. Skimming :

Sometimes one reads to get just a general idea of a certain reading material. In such a case, one lets his eyes pass over headlines, titles, sub- titles, topic sentences, conclusions and summaries. Such reading is used
when a reader does not need to examine a text thoroughly or his time
does not allow him to do so. We often skim in the case of newspapers, magazines, familiar books, stories, and the like. Thus skimming obviously contrasts with intensive reading and SQ3R in respect of the degree of con- centration involved in the reading process.

V. 5. Reading Stages :

Classroom reading normally goes through the stages of pre-reading, reading , and post-reading :

1. Pre-reading. The first stage in classroom reading is pre-reading, wherein the teacher prepares the class for reading a certain passage by teaching new words and new patterns that appear in that passage.
2. Reading. After the preparation done in the pre-reading stage, students read the passage silently for comprehension.
3. Post-reading. After silent reading, the teacher evaluates stu-
dents' comprehension through questions. In addition, this stage, i.e., post- reading, may include a variety of activities such as model reading, reading aloud, and questions asked by students.

V. 6. Planning a Reading Lesson :

Most or all foreign-language lessons for beginners normally centre
around the reading material. This means that in a reading lesson we do

not teach reading only. In fact, all the skills of language are to be taught
in the reading lesson. The plan of a reading lesson may contain the fol- lowing items :

1. Greeting. The first thing a teacher may do when he enters the classrooms is to greet the class.

2. Chalkboard Information. Then the teacher may write on the chalkboard some pieces of useful information in the foreign language such
as day, date, lesson number, part number ,and page. Such information
will be needed during the period and the teacher will save himself a lot of trouble if he writes such information on the chalkboard right at the beginning.

3. checking homework. The third item is that the teacher checks
the previous homework. This checking is important, because without it
students will come to the conclusion that their teacher gives homework
but does not follow it up. Then this conclusion is reached and confirmed, students will hesitate to do the assigned homework later. The homework
may be corrected after putting model answers on the chalkboard : each student will correct his own homework. The teacher, however, is supposed to examine the students' homework copybooks from time to time.

4. Review. After checking homework, the teacher reviews the old material of the previous lesson or lessons regarding content, vocabulary, patterns, spelling, and other language components.

5. New vocabulary. After reviewing, the teacher presents the new words of the lesson or the part he has planned to teach. Of course, the teacher's presentation if followed by students' practice.

6. New structures. In addition, the teacher presents to his class the new grammatical structures of the new lesson or part. His presentation is to be followed by appropriate drills.

7. Silent reading. After the preparation for reading secured by the previous two steps, students are told to read the new passage silently.

8. Comprehension questions. After silent reading, the teacher asks students some questions on the passage content to evaluate their ability
to comprehend what they have read.

9. Model reading. Then the teacher may read the passage aloud
with students listening or repeating to give them an example they should

imitate while reading aloud.

10. Reading aloud. After the teacher's model reading, students read
the passage aloud and individually.

11. Textbook exercises. Then the class may do some of the exer- cises on words or patterns usually included in the reading textbook.

12. Writing. Some minutes are devoted for writing, which may be handwriting, copying, dictation, or writing an exercise already done orally.

13. Assignment. The period ends with the teacher assigning for written homework something done in class orally.

However, the teacher should feel free to omit some of these steps if he finds that time does not allow him to do all of them or if he chooses to emphasize a limited number of goals at a certain period. Moreover, the teacher may modify the order of some steps when there is a good reason for that or when such modification does not contradict the logical or educational sequence of those steps.

V. 7. Reading Problems :

Reading is a complex activity that involves many elements, each of which may be a source of problems for readers :

1. Imperfect fit. English somehow suffers from a main defect, i.e.,
the imperfect fit between graphemes and phonemes. The same grapheme
may have more than one pronunciation, which may lead to occasional mis- pronunciation. In addition, the same phoneme may be represented by
more than one grapheme, which may lead to occasional misspelling.

2. Arabic-English graphic contrast. The two languages, Arabic and English, differ in the form or alphabet and the direction of writing and reading. English is read from the left side to the right side, whereas Ara- bic is read in the opposite direction. This requires some kind of eye re- training or adjustment on the part of the Arab student. Whose eye is accustomed to right-left movements while reading Arabic and has to adapt itself to left-right movements while reading English.

3. Vocabulary. Another reading problem is grasping the meaning of lexical items, i.e., words. The existence of many unfamiliar words in a
text makes it quite difficult to comprehend. This accounts for the

pre-reading stage, where students are prepared for reading by teaching
them new words.

4. Grammar. A student may sometimes find himself unable to
understand a sentence although he knows the meanings of all the words
in that sentence. His inability to get the meaning here may be attributed
to his failure to see the syntactic relations among the words within a cer- tain sentence. To put
it differently, the difficulty here is caused by the grammatical structure.

5. Content. It may occur that although a reader knows the words
and the patterns of a text, he may not understand it fully owing to the dif- faculty or
strangeness of content. In other words, the nature of the topic may be a problem in some cases.

6. Culture. The foreign culture may appear in some kinds of texts especially those dealing
with humanities. Since a foreign culture is usu-
ally unfamiliar to most learners, its abundance in a reading text may hinder adequate grasping
of meaning.

V. 8. Improvement of Reading :

There are several techniques that help in improving reading concerning both speed and comprehension :

1. Dictionary usage. Students must trained at the proper time to use dictionaries so as to
look up meanings, pronunciations, derivations, or spel- ling. This necessities teaching them the
ordered sequence of the alphabet
and how dictionary entries are arranged.

2. Reading patterns. The regularities of English must be emphasized at the early stages of learning this language. This implies that
beginners should be first exposed to reading selections that show a perfect correspondence between their written expressions and sound expres-
sions such as hit, sit, fit, nit, let, wet, set, top, dog, lot, and many other words. Patterns can also
be built into some reading habits through impli-
cit and later explicit generalizations, e.g., hid, hide, bit, bite, sit, site, and rid, ride.

3. Speed development. To develop the speed of reading, the teacher is urged to limit the time
given to students to read a certain passage. Reading under such a pressure of time gradually
trains students to adjust their eye movements, minimize eye fixation and eye regression, modify
their reading

habits, and widen the eye span. All these adjustments and up with a substantial speeding-up or reading without sacrificing comprehension.

4. Derivatives. To increase the student's vocabulary, the teacher
may teach the main derivatives of a new word such as the noun, verb, adverb, and adjective. Further, the teacher may give the synonym, the antonym, or both for a certain word. However, how much of these to offer depends on the learners' age and level.

5. Flash cards. Flash cards are another techniques that may be used to increase the reading speed and habituate the eye to catching larger
units at one glance instead of reading word by word or, still worse, letter
by letter. Flash cards, as it was explained before, are a pedagogical appli- cation of the gestalt theory of learning and the global theory on reading.
The eye span has to be a fairly large sequence of words perceived as a whole at one look.

6. Paragraph build-up. If students are guided to see how a good paragraph is usually structured, this will certainly facilitate their under- standing of paragraphs, which results in a gain in both comprehension and speed. A typical paragraph normally starts with a topic sentence, which,
as its name shows, tells the reader about the main theme or topic of that paragraph. Then the topic sentence is usually followed by some major supporting sentences, which illustrate the topic sentence. Each major sup- porting sentence is directly followed by one minor supporting sentence or more, the function of which is to illustrate the preceding major supporting sentence.

7. Logical relationships. If students are oriented to the variety of possible relationships among sentences within a single paragraph, this
will develop their abilities to comprehend reading passage accurately and easily. These relationships may involve comparison, contrast, definition, evaluation, evidence, cause, result, example, generalization, question, sum- mary, answer, reference, or restatement.

V. 9. Discussion :

1. Which method, in your opinion, is best for teaching reading to beginners ?

2.   What ways can you think of to improve reading other than those mentioned in this chapter ?

3. What reading problems may exist in addition to those problems discussed in this chapter ?

4. What type of reading is needed most in actual life ? What are the educational implications ?

5. What is the normal structure of an effective paragraph ?

6. How do you plan a reading lesson in the intermediate stage ?

TEACHING WRITING

Writing is usually one of the major skills involved in learning a foreign language, because it is one medium of conveying language. This chapter
will present the different stages of teaching writing starting from the
stage of pre-handwriting and ending with the stage of free writing. Further, this chapter will suggest a plan for a writing lesson.

VI. 1. Gradation :

Teaching the writing skill should be graded like all educational pro- cesses. The principle of gradation implies that teaching a certain program should proceed in accordance with a carefully designed plan and
should start with the easiest part of the learning material and gradually
move to more complicated parts.

If the gradation principle is applied to writing, one should start with teaching handwriting and then successively and cumulatively go to copying, dictation, controlled writing, and finally free writing. To put it diffe-
rently, writing is to start with letters, then words, sentences, paragraphs,
and at last long compositions.

Such gradation is necessary for at least two reasons. The first reason
is an educational one. By gradation we ensure that learning experiences
go from the easy to the difficult. The second reason is a logical one.
For example, we cannot teach writing a paragraph before teaching students to write a sentence. Similarly, we cannot teach students how to
write a long composition, *i.e.*, a multi- paragraph composition, before we teach them how to
write a single paragraph.

Another implication of graded writing is cumulativeness. This means
that when we teach the skill of copying, for example, and then move to dictation. The second
does not take the place of the previous one but it is added to it. Similarly, when free writing
starts, it does not excluded pre- vious steps but it is added to them.

VI. 2. Pre-writing :

The first stage in teaching writing is to teach handwriting, which may
be called the pre-writing stage. In this stage, learners are to be trained to write the graphic
symbols of the foreign language. i.e., its graphemes or alphabet. While teaching handwriting,
the teacher is expected to notice
the following :

1. There is a preliminary stage that precedes handwriting proper.
This stage may be referred to as the pre-handwriting stage, where begin- ners are trained the
draw straight, curved, and complex lines in certain mo- deled shapes. The purpose of these
exercises is to train the learner to control his manual movements as to line length and line
direction.

2. Beginners are to be guided to catch the pen or pencil properly, because some learners may
develop bad habits if left without observation
or guidance.

3. It is also important to make sure that students sit in the right manner with the copybook
in front of them in the right position.

4. The letters of the alphabet may be graded according to their dif- faculty. It may be more
convenient to start with straight –line letters such
as i, l, v, w, and x. Then students practice curved-line letters such as o
and c. finally, they practice complex or combined letters, *i.e.*, letters com- posed of straight and
curved lines, such as b, d, g, and q

5. The student must trained to unify the sizes of letters of the
same status. This means that all capital letters should be of the same
size and so should all small letters.

6. All letters should be written in the same slant.

7. All letters within a word should be equally spaced.

8. All words within a sentence should be equally spaced as well.

9. Students should be trained to write in straight, horizontal, and parallel lines.

10. Students are to be trained to write cursively.

11. Initial handwriting drills are to be written in pencil, and not in ink, because beginners frequently make mistakes and want to erase them.

VI. 3. Copying :

After mastering the alphabet of the foreign language. students are
required to copy familiar passages, i.e., passages they have already read. Copying can serve several purposes :

1. Copying is an exercise in handwriting.

2. It develops learners' consciousness of spelling.

3. It helps in focusing learners' attention on capitalization and punc- tuition.

4. It reinforces previously learned words and patterns.

VI. 4. Dictation :

The stage that follows copying is dictation, which is essential for the development of spelling consciousness in learners. However, dictation
exercises may accompany copying exercises.
The dictation material is preferably a previously read material. It is
also advisable that the teacher assigns a passage to be prepared at home for dictation in the coming class period. This is because the main goal is
to teach students and not to corner them through a dictation exercise
they have not prepared themselves for.
Concerning the role of dictation in learning a foreign language, it does not help in the development of spelling only, but in the development of
most language skills as well. First of all, it reinforces the learner's
ability to recognize sounds and phonemes contrasts. Therefore, dictation
trains the ear to distinguish phonemes upon hearing them. Besides, dicta- tion may also reinforce both punctuation and grammar.

A dictation exercise may follow these steps:

1.   The teacher assigns a familiar passage to be prepared at home for dictation.

2.   The teacher dictates to his class the whole assigned passage or some selected sentences or words. Each dictated unit has to be repeated three times at a fairly slow speed. The teacher has to pay additional atten- tion to the accuracy and clarity of his pronunciation while dictating because what and how he says determines what students will write.

3.   After dictating comes to an end, correction starts. In fact, the shorter the time between dictation and correction is, the better it will be because feed-back will be made close to the attempt itself.

4. Model answers are written on the chalkboard by students or the teacher.

5.   Each student may check his own exercise. Students may exchange copybooks and check one another's exercise. In some cases, the teacher
may collect the exercise copybooks to do the correction by himself or
check students' corrections. However, this technique of self-correction,
by which each student checks his own exercise, has often proved to be successful and motivating. Further, it saves the teacher's time and effort
and secures instant feed-back.

6. The teacher is expected to discuss common mistakes with his
class.
7. Every student is required to write his mis-spelled words in their correct forms three to five times each.

In brief, a dictation exercise passes through the steps of preparation, dictation, correction, discussion, and finally re-writing.

Moreover, to help students improve their spelling, they may be pro- vided with some spelling generalizations on condition that these genrali- zations are given to the suitable level of students and in suitable doses.
Here are some examples of spelling generalizations, which have proved
to be helpful to students :

1. Nouns ending in *s,x,z,sh,or,ch* take *–es* in the plural, e.g., *class, box, fez, brush*, and *watch*.

2. If a word ends in *y* preceded by a consonant and a suffix is added, *y* is changed into i, e.g., city +es ➡ cities, carry +ed ➡ carried.

3. If a word ends in silent e and a suffix starting with a vowel is added, e is usually dropped, e.g., *write+ing*► *writing, come+er*—► *comer.*

4. If a word ends in one consonant preceded by one stressed short vowel and a suffix starting with a vowel is added, the final consonant is doubled, e.g., *run+er* ►*runner* , *hot+est* ►*hottest.*

5. If a word begins with the same consonant a prefix ends in, both consonants remain, e.g., *dis+satisfied*► *dissatisfied, un+necessary* ——► *unnecessary.*

6. If *all* is combined with another word, one *I* is dropped, e.g., *all+ready* ——►*already,* *all+together* ——► *altogether.*

7. If *full* is combined with another word, one I is dropped, e.g., *hand+full* ——► *handful,* *care+full* ——► *careful.*

These are just examples of spelling generalizations, which have proved to be practically helpful to learners. Their helpfulness is strengthened by the high frequency of the cases where such generalizations are applicable.

VI. 5. Controlled Writing :

After the stages of handwriting, copying, and dictation, controlled writing may be started. This stage, i.e., controlled writing or guided writing , as it is sometimes called, contrasts with the following stage of free writing. In controlled writing students are usually provided with the needed content words, whereas in free writing content words are mainly produced by the students themselves.

Controlled writing may take any of following forms:

1. Parallel sentences. A model sentence is given and a group of content words is supposed to be patterned after that model. For example, *He cleans the car every day* may be the model sentence. The group of substi- tutes may be Mary, house, and morning. The parallel sentence will be *Mary* cleans the house every morning. Un this exercise, the student is supplied with content words and the pattern. What he is supposed to do is only to put some words in the place of other words and this is why such writing is called controlled or guided.

2. Parallel paragraphs. In the previous exercise, the model was a

sentence. In this exercise, the model is a paragraph. Some words are given to replace others in the model paragraph and a new paragraph gram- matically parallel to the model is to be written including the given substi- tutes.

3. Missing words. A passage or isolated sentences are given with some missing words, which are often of the grammatical type such as relatives, conjunctions and prepositions. Students are required to supply the sentences with those missing words.

4. Word ordering. A group of words is given and they are to be ordered to make a complete sentences ,e.g., speak he Chinese can fluently
——▶he can speak Chinese fluently or can he speak Chinese fluently?

5. Sentence ordering. A group of sentences is given in a haphat- zard order and they are to be re-arranged temporally, spatially, or logically to build one paragraph or more. In this exercise, the student does not pro- dce any words or patterns. He only understands the given sentences and their semantic or logical relationships and orders them accordingly.

6. Joining sentences. A group of simple sentences is give. They are to be joined together into a limited number of compound, complex, or compound-complex sentences probably to form a paragraph or more. The connectors may be provided by the exercise or required to be produced by students. This depends on the difficulty degree of the exercise, which in its turn depends on the students' level.

7. Sentence completion. One clause of a complex sentence is given and it may be the main or the subordinate one. Students are required to supply the missing clause that suits the situation semantically and grammatically, e.g., If you ask your teacher, _____.

These seven types are just examples of exercises that may be given under controlled writing. The list of controlled exercises may include dozens of different types. In fact, all the exercises discussed in the chap- ter of «Teaching Grammar »in the section of «Grammar Exercises» may be considered as exercises of controlled writing.

Controlled writing mainly aims at training students to build sen- tences through imitation, substitution, ordering, transformation, and other means. However, controlled writing should not be emphasized at the expense of free writing because the two activities, though related, are quite different.

VI. 6. Free Writing :

After about three years of learning a foreign language in a normal school program, students are expected to start free writing. In the first
three years, students practice handwriting, copying, dictation, and controlled writing. Afterwards, free writing is added to go hand in hand with dictation and controlled writing.

VI. 6. 1. Mechanics of Free Writing :

ics, which include the following :

1. Margin. An inch-wide margin is to be left preferably on both sides of the page. Such margins will be needed for the teacher's com- ments on the student's composition.

2. Date. Students are instructed on where and how to write the date in the foreign language.

3. Title. Students are to be taught how and where to put down the title of the composition. This involves teaching which words in the title
have to be initially capitalized and which words have to be written in initial small letters. The first word and the last one in the title are capita- lized. Concerning medial words, they are capitalized if they are content words and not capitalized if they are function ones.

4. Indentation. Students are to be instructed to leave a nearly-inch-wide space at the beginning of every paragraph.

5. Where to write. Students are to be given clear instructions on whether they will write on the right-hand page or the left-hand one, on both pages of each sheet or one page, on every line or every other line, in pen- cil or ink, and so on. The teacher should also instruct them on where to
do their re-writing of their composition after correction.

Although such matters may seem to be unimportant, they are actually of special importance. For example, if students are not given clear and strict instructions on how and where to write and how to arrange their writing, the teacher may find compositions written on every line, without

margins, or with very narrow ones. In such case, the teacher will find it difficult to record his comments and corrections of the composition. Further, without indentation, it will be also difficult to see where a paragraph begins or ends.

It is, necessary to remember that once certain instructions are given by the teacher to his class, he must always insist on sticking to them. Repeated lenience concerning instructions often tempts many students not to abide by them, which ends up with more difficulties for the teacher himself in correcting students' writing.

VI. 6. 2. Composition Topics :

Composition may be classified into different types with regard to topic or content :

1. Descriptive writing. A descriptive composition is just an account of the described thing. Such an account may be factual or imaginative. The tense of verbs is usually present simple : however, they may be past simple if the described thing is no more existent. Descriptive topic- may be the easiest types to begin free writing with.

2. Narrative writing. Narration is simply telling a story. The se- quence of ideas here is normally chronological and verbs are usually in the past tense. Of course, the story may be factual or imaginative and thus it is similar to description in this respect.

3. Expository writing. The purpose of expository writing is to ex- plain and clarify ideas directly through definition, analysis, comparison, or information.

4. Persuasive writing. The purpose of persuasive writing is to emotion- ally persuade or rationally convince the reader of a certain opinion.
5. Precis .Precis is a kind of summary. It requires concentrated read- ing, disciplined thinking, and accurate writing.

All these types of writing may be practiced in the secondary stage, i.e., after three or four years of foreign-language learning within a school program. Description and narration may be emphasized at the beginning, whereas exposition and persuasion may be added later. Concerning pre- cis, it may accompany all the other types with proper attention to the dif- ficulty level of the passage to be summarized.

First of all, the teacher himself has to know the characteristics of an effective paragraph. The reason is obvious: he cannot teach his students how to write good paragraphs if he himself does not know those qualifies. There- fore, it is advisable that the teacher exposes his students to model paragraphs and helps them to analyse such paragraphs so as to let them get a clear idea of the factors that secure paragraph effectiveness. Here is a brief discussion of those main factors :

1. Unity. The unity of a paragraph means that all the sentences of the paragraph serve the same purpose and centre around the same topic. In other words, all sentences within a paragraph pour into the central idea of the topic sentence, which is illustrated by some following major sup- porting sentences, each of which is illustrated by some following minor supporting sentences. This paragraph unity may be established through careful pre-outlining. An outline is a plan of ideas to be included in a para- graph and it is to be schemed before actual writing starts.

2. Coherence. The second characteristic of an effective paragraph is coherence, which means that the sentences within a paragraph stick together in a way that marks the progress of thought. This is attained through the organization of ideas and through linking devices, which may be automatic or deliberate. One way of automatic linking is repeating a content word in two or more consecutive sentences. Concerning deli- berate devices, they may be general nouns such as theory, suggestion, and opinion or meaning links such as further, however, major, in brief, and as a result. These devices cannot sentences within a paragraph in a way that makes it easy for the reader to follow the sequence of the writer's thinking and to grasp the semantic and logical relationships among sen- tences.

3. Emphasis. It is conscious ordering of ideas, which can be secured through careful outlining ad careful writing. The order of ideas may follow any of these patterns: chronological order, spatial order, the cause than the effect, advantages then disadvantages or vice versa, instances than generali- zations, the general then the specific. To put it differently, the ideas of a paragraph may be ordered chronologically, spatially, or logically.

4. Clarity. Clarity can be attained through several ways. Firstly, terms

have to be defined so as to limit their indication. Secondary, writing should suit the reader's level in terms of style, structures, content, and vocabulary. Thirdly, the writer's hand should co with his mind: no wide jumps to conclusions are made. Fourthly, the writer should avoid all sorts of lexical and grammatical ambiguities.

5. Correctness. Correctness is simply obeying the regulations of the correct usage of language.

In brief, unity means the oneness of thought in all sentences within a paragraph; coherence, the linking of sentences; emphasis, the ordering of sentences; clarify, the elimination of ambiguities; correctness, slocking to the habits of language. Of course, knowing these qualities a good paragraph
will not make a person a famous paragrapher. Nerveless, knowing them
helps a person develop his writing skill more easily because he will be con- scios of what makes a paragraph an effective one.

VI. 6. 4. A Long Composition :

In a six-year foreign language program, a long composition will be the culminating stage in writing, because it is in fact the most difficult skill if compared to other writing skills. A long composition refers to a composition of two paragraphs or more.

This means that long compositions may be written in the last two
years in a six-year program. Further, the factors that secure the effective- ness of a long composition are the same ones that secure the effective- ness of a paragraph; unity of each paragraph and unity of all paragraphs, intra-paragraph coherence and inter-paragraph coherence, clarity, emphasis, and correctness.

In school programs such as those in the Arab countries. English as a foreign language is generally taught for six years. Students in the fifth
year are to be trained to write two-paragraph compositions and students
in the sixth year of the program are to be trained to write three-paragraph compositions. It is advised that the teacher analyses with his class some models of long compositions before they start practicing them.

VI. 7. Writing Scheme :

Now that we have discussed the different stages of writing .let us see how each stage can fit into a general scheme within the foreign language prog- ramme.

This distribution of writing skills may be shown in this table, where the horizon- tal headings refer to the writing skills graded according to their difficulty and where the vertical headings refer to the six years of the foreign language program. In this table, the symbol S indicates that a certain writing skill is started in a certain year in the program. The symbol C indicates that a certain skill is continued in that year. If the skill is not practiced in a certain year, a dash appears in that slot.

	Hand-writing	Copy-ing	Dict-ation	Con-trolled writing	One para-graph	Two para-graph	Three para-graphs	Precis
1st year	S	S	—	—	—	—	—	—
2nd year	C	C	S	S	—	—	—	—
3rd year	—	C	C	C	—	—	—	—
4th year	—	—	C	C	S	—	—	S
5th year	—	—	C	C	C	S	—	C
6th year	—	—	C	C	C	C	S	C

This table illustrates the following points :

1. In the first year of the foreign language program, handwriting is started and copying follows.

2. In the second year, handwriting and copying continue; dictation and controlled writing start.

3. In the third year, handwriting comes to an end; copying, dicta-tion, and controlled writing continue.

4. In the fourth year, copying is stopped; dictation and controlled writing continue; one-paragraph composition and précis start.

5. In the fifth year, dictation, controlled writing, one-paragraph com- postion, and précis continue; two-paragraph composition starts.

6. In the sixth year, dictation, controlled writing, one-and-two-para- graph composition, and précis continue; three-paragraph composition starts.

In terms of writing skills, the table also shows the following points:

1. Handwriting starts in the first year of the foreign-language prog- ram and continues in the second year only.

2. Copying starts in the first year and continues for two more years.

3. Dictation starts in the second year and continues till the end of the program.

4. Controlled writing starts in the second year and continues all through the program.

5. One-paragraph free writing starts in the forth year and continues all through till the end of the program.

6. Two-paragraph free writing starts in the fifth year and continues in the following year.

7. Three-paragraph free writing starts in the last year of the program.

8. Precis starts in the fourth year and continues for two years more.

VI. 8. Focused Method :

The focused method may be used in teaching free writing. According to this method, each composition period has a specific goal, on which the teacher focuses in his teaching and later his correction.

The possible list of such goals may look like this :
1. outline
2. title
3. margin
4. indentation
5. date
6. handwriting
7. topic sentences
8. supporting sentences
9. unity
10. linking devices
11. vocabulary
12. spelling
13. punctuation
14. grammatical structures
15. ordering ideas
16. Clarity

The teacher focuses on one goal or more in each period. However, in the following period, previously-achieved goals are added to the new goal. In other words, goals are approached and retained in a cumulative manner.

The focused method has several advantages:

1. Grading the student depends on taught material and not on the student's chronic weaknesses.

2. This method takes into consideration the teacher's limited time since the teacher focuses on one goal each time.

3. The complex skill of free writing is broken into learnable units.

4. The teacher ceases to be an error hunter.

5. Progress in writing becomes measurable and goals become more achievable.

6. The method is somehow programmed and the teaching material is carefully graded.

VI. 9. A Writing-Lesson Plan :

When a free-writing lesson is to be planned, the teacher may follow these steps : preparation, writing, correction, and re-learning. In the com- ing sections, we shall discuss each step in some detail.

VI. 9. 1. Preparation :

Before students start writing freely on a certain topic, the teacher should prepare them for such writing o as to minimize their mistakes and train them how to handle tasks fairly successfully. For this preparation, the teacher is advised to consider these suggestions:

1. Remind your class of the mechanics of writing such as margin, date, title, and indentation.
2. Let students be acquainted with the factors of effective writing through the analysis of some model paragraphs and long compositions.
3. Help your students to set an outline before they start writing. Such outlining is necessary for securing unity and emphasis.

4. Lead some oral discussion on the topic especially when the main aim is teaching and not testing.

5. Supply the class with key words they need for writing on a cer- tain topic.

6. Remember that the composition content should be both interest- ing and within the students' level.

7. Provide students with helpful restrictions on the number of para- graphs they are required to write, the number of words, sentences, or lines. You may give them the topic sentence of each paragraph. Further, you may guide them to suitable verb tenses. These quantitative and quali- tative restrictions make free writing somehow controlled or guided.

VI. 9. 2. Actual Writing :

After students are prepared, as has been explained in the previous sec- tion, they start writing a draft copy first and then the final copy. It is generally better to let students write their compositions in the classroom and not at home, because in the case of home writing many students will persuade parents, other relatives, or friends to do the writing for them. Further, some students will do no writing at all :they just copy other classmates' comosi- tions. When this occurs, many students lose the opportunity of real practice and will be deceiving themselves and their teachers.

VI. 9. 3. Correction :

When actual writing comes to an end, the teacher collects copybooks for correction, which may take one of the following forms :

1. Error hunting. The teacher may correct all mistakes made by the student. However: this method of correction may cause some negative side effects. A student who sees that almost every word he has written has been red-marked by the teacher becomes quite frustrated and forms a conclusion that he will never write correctly. Such a conclusion usually ends up with despair and losing the motive for learning or progress.

2. Selective correction. In this method, the teacher does not cor- rect all mistakes. He only selects some of them and especially those big ones. This method saves the teacher's time and effort and may motivate students better.

3. Symbolized correction. The   first two methods deal with the quantity of mistakes to be corrected. On the other hand, this method and the next one deal with how to correct regardless of quantity. In symbol-

lized correction, the teacher underlines the mistake without writing the

correct alternative. He only writes a symbol such as I, P, G, S, or V, which tells the student that he made a mistake in indentation, punctuation,

grammar, spelling, or vocabulary. The student himself is expected to dis- cover the correct alternative with the teacher's guidance.

4. Detailed correction. In detailed correction, the teacher under-

lines the mistake and writes down the correct alternative in detail.

VI. 9. 4. Re-learning :

While correcting students' writing, the teacher is expected to make a

list of common errors. In the next period, he should do the following as a part of a re-teaching process, which may lead to re-learning :

1. He should discuss common mistakes with his class.

2. He should re-teach areas that require re-teaching. What areas to be re-taught depends on what students' writing reveals.

3. Students are required to re-write the composition in its correct

form.

VI. 10. Discussion :

1. How is the gradation principle applied to writing ?

2. Give twenty different exercises on controlled writing with at least

two sentences in each exercise.

3. Give ten more spelling generalizations with five examples in each case.

4. What are the qualities of an effective paragraph ?

5. Write a model paragraph of your own on any topic you choose. Show how it is built up and how its effectiveness is achieved.

6. Think of five topics suitable for the secondary stage. If three para- graphs are to be written on each topic, suggest a topic sentence for each paragraph.

7. Set an outline of a three-paragraph composition on any topic you choose and then write those paragraphs.

LANGUAGE TESTING

Testing plays a major role in teaching: good testing is essential for
good teaching and good learning especially in normal school programs. Experience has shown that both teachers and students emphasize what
tests emphasize. In consequence, if there is a leak in the testing system, this will cause leaks in the processes of teaching and learning.

In this chapter, we shall discuss the purposes of tests, their different types, what language areas to test, and how to test each area. Further, we shall discuss how to make a test, how to give it, and the conditions of a good test.

VII. 1. Purposes of Testing :

Although most students and some teachers dislike tests, the need for testing is great. Tests can serve more than one purpose :

1. Achievement. A test may be used to measure students' achieve- ment. The student usually desires to know how much he has achieved
and where he stands among his classmates. Test scores may urge a stu- dent to compete with others or with himself. A low sore may motives a student to double his effort to improve his own achievement. A high score gives him a feeling of satisfaction and his success will lead him to further success.

2. Self-evaluation. The teacher needs tests to evaluate his own teaching. He likes to know how much of his teaching has resulted in learning. If the test is well-designed, scores do have an implication. Their

highness most probably indicates effective teaching and their lowness
indicates there is something wrong somewhere. In the later case, the
teacher perhaps needs to modify his methods or re-teach.

3. Experimentation. Tests are also used in educational experi- ments. If we want to compare two methods and determine which teaching method leads to better learning, a pre-test is given to the controlled group and the experimental group. At the termination of the experiment,
the same test is repeated. Pre-test scores and post-test scores are entered into certain statistical formulas to check the significance of differences
between the two groups of scores.

4. Promotion. Tests are needed to determine which students
deserve to be promoted from a grade to a higher one. Without testing, pro- motion will be automatic or impressionistic, which is either impractical or unfair.

5. Parents' information. Parents want to know how their children
are progressing, where they are weak or good, and what help they are in need of. All this information is provided to parents through tests.

6. Diagnosis. Sometimes the test aims at diagnosing problem
areas. This diagnosis can be achieved through computing the index of dif- faculty for each item in the test. Such computation can show us which
items are easy, which ones are difficult, and which ones are very difficult
for those students. In the light of this classification, the teacher can vary emphasis depending on the difficulty level of each learning area.

7. Grouping. Tests are needed to group students homogenously
in schools that classify students of the same grade into levels and make each classroom contain only those students who belong to a certain level.
Of course, such grouping mainly depends on the results of tests.

8. Urge. It is unfortunately true that many students study mainly because the tests. In fact, many students, if not the majority, do not study unless a test is announced. For such students, tests are probably the sole motive for working hard.

9. Prognosis. A test may be used to predict whether a certain stu- dent can potentially succeed in a certain study program. Each score on
that test has a certain interpretation derived from repeated observation of many cases of correlation between present prognostic-test scores and
future achievement scores.

10. Entrance. Many educational institutes do not admit students except after screening them through an entrance examination. Their scores on this examination determine whether they will be accepted or rejected by that institute.

11. Remedy. A test may be used to select those students who need special treatment so as to remedy their weakness at a certain area of knowledge.

12. Placement. A test is sometimes used to know the level of a student transferred from another country or institute of a different educa- tional system. Such a test will help in placing that student in the grade that suits his level of achievement.

Of course, these functions of tests apply to all subjects including the foreign language. Further, the same test may perform several functions simultaneously. For example, a test that measures students' achievement may be used the teacher in self-evaluation as well. It may be also used as a promotion criterion and to provide parents with information about their children.

VII. 2. Test Types :

Tests may be classified into many types: here are some major ones :

1. Objective tests. A test is objective if its grading is independent of the person marking that test. There is usually a key of answers that leaves no room for subjectivity in grading. A typical example of objective tests in multiple choice tests or false-true tests.

2. Subjective tests. A test is subjective if the score depends on the marker. In subjective tests, it usually happens that different markers give different scores. The gap between the markers may be sometimes very wide. Such tests contrast with objective ones. A typical example of subjective tests is the test on free writing.

3. Speed tests. A speed test aims at measuring the speed of per- formance. In this case, the test is made a little longer than the time given. For example, a test may consist of two hundred items on grammar to be answered in one hour.

4. Achievement tests. An achievement test aims at measuring stu- dents' achievement. In this case, the given time is made to be adequate,

because the emphasis here is on measuring achievement and not speed. Therefore, achievement tests contrast with speed ones.

5. Public tests. If the test is prepared by a central authority and given on a country-wide scale, it is a public test. It is usually announced and relatively long. It is normally given at the end of a school cycle to decide which students deserve promotion to the higher cycle.

6. School tests. If the test is locally prepared and given at the school level by the class teacher, it is called a school test, which contrasts with a public test in terms of length, scale purpose, and examiner.

7. Standard tests. A standardized test is carefully designed one that has undergone long experimentation and research. Each score has a special interpretation that indicates where a certain scorer stands among a statistical population of similar individuals.

8. Normal tests. If the test is not standardized, it is a normal one. The majority of tests, of course, belong to this normal category.

9. Written tests. The answers here are to be given in a written form.

10. Oral tests. The answers here are to be given orally.

11. Announced tests. The teacher assigns the test material and fixes a certain date in advance.

12. Drop tests. In contrast with an announced test, a drop test is given without previous announcement. It is usually a short one and it aims at keeping students on the alert.

13. Classroom tests. The test questions are given and answered in class.

14. Home tests. In contrast with a classroom test, a home test is given in class but answered at home.

15. Closed-book tests. Textbooks are closed while students are taking the test.

16. Open-book tests. Students are allowed to use their books while answering the questions of a test.

In addition, one may notice that not all these types exclude one another.

For example, a test may fit in eight types at the same time : it may be an objective, achievement, local, normal, written, announced, classroom,
closed-book test without any inner contradictions of classification. On the
other hand, it is obvious that some types exclude one another. For ins- tance, a test cannot be announced and drop at the same time. Further, these types may be used in all school subjects including the foreign language.

VII. 3. What to test :

Concerning foreign language testing, tests should cover all the skills involved in learning a foreign language according to the objectives designed by a specific program. The involved areas are the following :

1. Pronunciation. Students are tested in producing and recognizing
the sounds of the foreign language.

2. Grammar. Students are tested to measure their abilities to pro- duce and understand grammatical structures.

3. Vocabulary. A vocabulary test aims at measuring the students' abilities to produce and understand the words of the target language.

4. Spelling. A spelling test measures the students' abilities to
spell the words they have learnt.

5. Handwriting. At the early stages of learning s foreign language, students' handwriting may be evaluated.

6. Aural comprehension. An aural comprehension test aims at measuring the students' ability to comprehend a passage through listening.

7. Visual comprehension. A visual comprehension test aims at measuring the student's ability to comprehend a passage through reading.

8. Composition. A composition test measures the student's ability
to write one paragraph or more on a certain topic.

9. Precis. A précis test measures both comprehension and writing, because a student is required first to understand a certain text and then summarize it within given limits.

10. Translation. A translation test involves understanding a text in
the native or foreign language and then expressing its ideas in the other

language. This means that translation may go in two directions : from the foreign language to the native one and vice versa.

11. Punctuation. A punctuation test requires supplying a written passage with the omitted punctuation marks.

12. speaking. A speech test aims at measuring the student's ability to speak the foreign language correctly and at a reasonable speed.

VII. 4. Testing Each Skill :

This section will show us how we may test each of the skills men- tioned in the previous section.

VII. 4. 1. Pronunciation Tests :

A pronunciation teats may include one or more of the following forms :

1. Reading aloud. A student may be asked to read aloud words, sentences, or passages that contain already taught material . To evaluate such a test objectively, a certain amount of marks may be subtracted for every mistake in pronunciation especially when the reading material is in the form of sentences or passages. This test may also evaluate the stu- dent's intonation and stresses.

2. Auditory discrimination. The teacher pronounces a list of words in pairs while students are listening. The student is required to write *I* if the two words of the pare are identically pronounced or *D* if the two words are differ- ently pronounced. In other words, *I* means that the second word of the pair is just a repetition of the first word and *D* means that the pair contains two different words. Such a test measures the student's ability to recognize the phonemes of the foreign language especially those that do not exist in the native language or those that have a different status in each language.

3. Visual discrimination. This test of visual discrimination is simi- lar to the test of auditory discrimination. However, in visual discrimia- tion, the pairs are only read by the examinee, whereas in auditory discrimi- nation the pairs are only heard by the examinee.

4. Underlined graphemes. In this test, a group of words is given with a letter or a cluster of letters underlined in each word. The under- lined letters are usually graphically identical but they are not necessarily

so. All the underlined letters in the group are pronounced in the same way except one letter, which the student is required to recognize. For example, in the group *child, chimney, chemistry, chin*, all the italicized clusters are pronounced /č/ except the third cluster. In the word che- mistry, which is pronounced /k/.

5. Phonemic transcription. In advanced levels, a student may be asked to transcribe words, sentences, or passages phonemically or even phonetically.

VII. 4. 2. Grammar Tests :

Grammatical structures may be tested in different ways:

1. Form modification. A bracketed word is required to be put in its correct form, e.g., he (come) to school tomorrow.

2. Filling in spaces. A word, normally a structural one, is missing from a sentence and is to be supplied, e.g., they _____ just arrived.

3. Synthesis. Two simple sentences or more are to be synthesized into one compound or complex sentence.

4. Error location. The student is asked to underline any grammatical mistakes in a sentence and re-write the sentence in its correct form.

5. Completion. One clause of a complex sentence is given and the other is to be supplied. Such a test measures the student's ability to see the semantic and structural relationships between the main clause and the subordinate one within the same sentence.

6. Translation. A sentence in a certain form is to be changed into another specified form, e.g., direct speech into indirect speech, an active voice into a passive voice, statements into questions, statements into imperatives, and vice versa.

7. Multiple choice. This is a recognition test, where two or more answers are given for each test item, only one of which is correct. The student is to select and encircle the correct answer, e.g., this is the friend   [which, who, whom, when] arrives last night.

8. Parallel structure. A group of words is to be concatenated in a way to parallel another sentence in terms of grammatical structure.

9. Word re-arrangement. A group of words is to be arranged in a way that

makes a grammatically acceptable sentence, e.g., the over he wall jumped.

As a matter of fact, the list may include more types. Each different grammar exercise may be a different grammar test. This is one of few
cases where exercises used for teaching are the same as those used for testing in terms of form and quality.

VII. 4. 3. Vocabulary Tests :

Vocabulary tests may aim at evaluating the student's ability to pro-
duce certain words or recognize those words. This implies that testing parallels teaching : as teaching may be for production or recognition, so
may testing be. Vocabulary tests may take the following forms:

1. Multiple choice. Several answers are given to fill in a blank.
The student is to choose the only correct answer, e.g., he went to see the football (competition, game, match, contest). Of course, such a test is one of recognition and not production.

2. Synonyms. A certain word is used in a context and the student
is required to give a synonymous word.

3. Antonyms. A certain word is used in a context and its opposite
is to be given according to the meaning of that word in that specific con- text.

4. Derivatives. A certain word in a sentence is underlined. Another sentence follows with a blank to be filled with a suitable word derived
from the underlined word in the first sentence, e.g., he is a generous man; his _____is known everywhere.

5. Matching. A list of words is given and the student is to find the meaning of each word in the first list in another list usually outnumbering
the first list.

6. Filling-in. a content word is missing in a certain sentence and is
to be supplied, e.g., hydrogen is a gas, but water is a _____. Such a test is a production one.

7. Aided filling-in. a content word is missing but some aid is given
to help the student recall that word. The aid may be the initial letter of the missing word, the final letter, or the number of the letters contained in
that word. Further, the aid may be two initial letters or more. It may be

also two or more final letters. Moreover, the aid may be both the initial and final letters.

VII. 4. 4. Spelling Tests :

Spelling tests may take the following forms :

1. Dictation. The teacher dictates to his class, slowly and clearly, selected words, sentences, or passages preferably already assigned.

2. Roots and affixes. A root is given with a prefix or suffix added.
The student is to combine the root and its affixes taking into consideration any probable changes in the spelling of the root, the affix, or both, e.g.,
in + regular, country+ s, spoon+ full.

3. Error detection. The test contains groups, each of which consists
of several words. One word in each group is misspelled. The student is
to underline this misspelled word and correct it.

4. Missing letter. A word is given with one letter missing. The stu- dent is to supply that missing letter Aids may be given in such a test. For example, the student is told to add a vowel to each word, a consonant, or one of a given list of letters. Such aid reduces the number of choices and thus increases the probability of correct answering. To make the test more difficult, the student is told to add a letter if necessary, which implies
that the student has to decide first whether there is any letter really mis- sing or not before he thinks of what letter to add.

5. Multiple choice. Each group of words consists of several words,
one of which is correctly spelled. The student is to encircle or underline
this correct word.

VII. 4. 5. Handwriting Tests :

Handwriting may be tested in different ways, which are used to evalu- ate a beginner's ability to shape letters correctly:
1. Small letters. The teacher pronounces some graphemes of the
foreign-language alphabet and students are required to write down those graphemes or letters in their small variety, i.e., small allograph. The pur- pose of such a test is to evaluate the beginner's ability to recognize phonemeg- rapheme associations.

2. Capital letters. This test is similar to the previous one in proce-

dure and purpose. The differences is in the allographs to be written by the student. In this test, the student is required to write the letters in their capital variety or capital allographs.

3. Imitation. In the imitation test , a model sentence in the students' books or on the chalkboard is to be limited repeatedly to evaluate the student's handwriting habits.

VII. 4. 6. Comprehension Tests:

A comprehension test aims at evaluating the student's ability to grasp the meanings and information offered in a passage perceived through lis- tening or reading. The passage has to be within the students' level. In other words, its words and structures have to be familiar to students. Comprehension tests may take several forms :

1. Questions. The passage is followed by written or oral questions that require written or oral answers. However, it must be noticed that such a test does not measure the comprehension ability only but the expression ability as well.

2. Multiple choice. The student is to recognize the correct answer from several alternatives. Such a test does not involve comprehending the text only, but the question and the given answers also. In other words, correct answering requires understanding the text itself and the evaluating material, *i.e.*, questions and answers.

3. True-false. This test requires determining whether a certain sta- tement is true or false according to the comprehension passage. If the test is to be made more difficult, the student is also required to consider if the statement is undetermined, which means that the passage does not supply the reader with information adequate to decide the truth or fal- sity of a specific statement. Another variety of this test demands the cor- rection of the statement if it is a false one.

4. Filling-in. sentences related to the comprehension passage are presented with some words missing. Students are asked to fill in the spaces according to the information offered in the passage. The missing words are to be of content or factual nature and not grammatical words because the purpose here is to test understanding content and not master- ing grammar.

5. Pairing. Two lists of incidents are given in the form of clauses,

phrases, or words. The student is supposed to choose and match with each incident in the first list another incident in the second list which is most associated with it. Of course, the listed incidents are taken from the com- prehension passage.

6. Ordering. A list of statements is given to the student, who should arrange those statements in the order of their occurrence according to the chronological facts of the comprehension passage.

VII. 4. 7. Composition Tests :

Composition tests may be in any of the following forms:

1. Students are asked to write on a certain topic absolutely freely, i.e., without any restriction on content, quantity, or form and without any aid whatsoever.

2. A certain topic is specified and the topic sentence of every para- graph is given to control the direction of the student's thinking.

3. Students are to write on a certain topic with quantitative limits assigned such as number of words, paragraphs, lines, or sentences.

4. A whole outline of a paragraph or a long composition may be sup- plied to students, who are expected to transform those headpoints or con- trolling ideas into a unified and coherent paragraph or long composition.

Concerning the grading of compositions, one may use the percent sys- tem, i.e., the one hundred system . An alternative is the letter system, *i.e.*, giving the grade in the form of letters such as A,B,C,D and E. The third alternative is the quality system, i.e., describing the composition as excellent, very good, good, fair, and not satisfactory. The fourth alternative is the pass-fail system, wherein a composition is either satisfactory or not.

The most common and practical system is the percent one. It allows the widest range of grades and thus can distribute students better than the other systems. It also lends itself easily to mathematical and statis- tical operations such as averaging and curve constructions. The letter and quality systems are in fact the same in essence since each classifies stu- dents into five categories. Concerning the pass- fail system, it may be the least efficient system if compared to other systems because the grad- ing alternatives are minimal in number.

VII. 4. 8. Precis Tests :

In précis tests, a passage is to be read carefully and then require- ments may take one of the following forms :

1. Students are required to answer the questions on the passage in complete sentences. The answers are to be arranged one after the other
to form a paragraph, which summarizes the main points or incidents in the original text. In such tests, the questions are phrased in a certain way that eliminates yes-no answers, because such answers do not fit a continuous paragraph. Further, such a test usually puts limits to the length of answers by giving the maximum number of words to be included in the sum- mary.

2. The test may be one question only, the answer of which makes a paragraph that covers some basic ideas of the text.

3. The test may just demand a summary of the text with some res- tractions pertaining to the permitted number of words, sentences, or para- graphs.

VII. 4. 9. Translation Tests :

Translation tests may take one of the following forms:

1. A passage in the foreign language is to be translated into the native language.

2. A passage in the native language is to be translated into the foreign language.

3. Instead of the passage, separate sentences may be given.

It must be noted that translation into the foreign language involves understanding the native-language text and expressing in the foreign lan- gugae. In contrast, translation into the native language involves under- standing the foreign-language text and expressing in the native language.

VII. 4. 10 Punctuation Tests :

A punctuation test may include4 one of these forms or more:

1. Students are asked to add a specific punctuation mark or more such as stops, commas, or inverted commas. In this case, the passage will

have all punctuation marks except the type or types to be added by stu- dents.

2.   Another way to test punctuation is to ask students to add all the necessary punctuation marks to a sentence or passage devoid of any marks without any indication of their positions.

3.   An easier test may limit the number of the missing punctuation marks. This will prevent a student from adding ten marks, for example,
then he should add five.

4.   The test may inform students of the position of the missing punc- tuition marks and requires the addition of the proper marks in those
assigned positions.

5.   The text to be punctuated may be individual sentences or a para- graph.

VII. 4. 11. Speech Tests :

The purpose of speech tests is to evaluate the student's ability to produce the foreign language orally, correctly, and fairly fluently. These tests may be in one of these forms:

1.   A student is asked to talk about a familiar topic for a limited dura- tion of time. The student is then evaluated for fluency and correctness.

2.   A student may be asked questions, each of which requires a brief answer of one sentence or two.

3.   The questions may be given by the teacher or through a tape with timed pauses between each question and the one that follows.

4.   The stimulus may be a picture, which the student is to describe
or comment on orally.

5.   Two students may be asked to participate in a normal conversa- tional situation, *i.e.*, a dialogue.

VII. 5. Making Tests :

When a test is to be made, the examiner is expected to note the following principles :

1.   It is very important to determine the objective or objectives of

the test. Without determining objectives, the test loses its function. Ob- jective determination involves the language skills to be evaluated, the dif- faculty level of the test, and the skill aspect, i.e., production or recognition.

2. Each item in the test must stick to those set objectives. Otherwise, the item loses validity, an essential characteristic of good testing.

3. The time allowed for taking the test should be adequate for ans- wering the questions. The teacher may check this adequacy by trying the
test and forming a rough idea about the needed time.

4. It is recommended to place easy items at the beginning of the test and let more difficult ones come later.

5. The test should include items varying in their degrees of difficulty
in order to spread students over a fairly wide range of scores and thus dis- criminate between slow students, average students, and bright students.

6. The teacher should in advance decide the weight of the test in relation to the final grade and inform students of this proportion.

7. He should also determine how he is going to grade the test. In other words, he should be clear on the weight of each item within the test itself.

8. It is advisable to let the maximal grade of each question appear
on the question sheet. This will help students very emphasis and plan time distribution according to the relative weight of each question.

9. The test should be clear in its questions and instructions on how
to answer. This clarity is essential for the test reliability.

10. The test should minimize the role of blind guessing in score attainment.

11. The test should represent the greatest part of the assigned mate- rial so as to be fair to students and eliminate dependence on mere luck.

12. If the examiner intends to penalize for wrong answers to discou- rag blind guessing, he must plan such penalty beforehand and let students know of it before they start answering.

VII. 6. Giving Tests :

The previous section deals with how to prepare a test: this section shows us how to give it. The teacher has to consider these points while giving a test :

1. It may be better to give some instructions before question sheets
are distributes such as how and where to answer.

2. The rest of the instructions are given immediately after distributing question sheets.
3. Students may be given a few minutes to ask about unclear points related to the test.
4. No questions are allowed after the first five minutes.

5. If there is a penalty for wrong answers, students have to be informed of it before starting.

6. Students should receive no help during taking the test because teaching takes place before and after the test but not during the test.

In addition, the teacher should insist on students' honesty while taking the test and prevent cheating because cheating can dispossess tests
of their functions and make them almost meaningless. To minimize cheat- ing, the teacher is advised to try the following suggestions:

1. It is better to space students if the size of the room allows.

2. The teacher may use two parallel forms of the same test or more. Parallel forms may be made by including test items identical in content but different in wording. Further, parallel forms may be made by including
items different in content but equal in difficulty.

3. The same test may be made into several forms by putting its
items in different arrangements.

4. It is better to stand in front of the class with minimal movement than to keep moving around among examinees.

5. Some students need to be reminded right at the beginning that cheating will be severely penalized.

6. Cheaters must be strictly dealt with because misplaced kindness usually spoils the educational process.

VII. 7. A Good Test :
A good test is characterized by the following qualities :

1. Validity. A valid test actually measures what it claims to mea-
sure. If a test aims at evaluating spelling, it becomes invalid if it evaluates pronunciation. However, *valid* and *invalid* are not absolute terms: a test valid for a certain purpose may be invalid for another.

2. Reliability. A reliable test is one that is dependable. In other
words, if the same test or a parallel one is taken again by the same stu- dents, the score average will be almost consonant provided that the time between the test and the re-test is of a reasonable length. Foe example, if the average of students' scores on a certain test is 80% and the average of the re-test scores drops down to 40% during a week's time. This may imply there is something wrong with the test itself.

3. Scorability. A scorable test lends itself to easy and accurate
marking without wasting too much time or effort.

4. Representativeness. A good test should include a representative sample of questions. In other words, it has to include items from different areas of the material assigned for the test.

5. Discrimination. A discriminative test should be able to distinguish among the different levels of students. For example, if all students
score between 80% and 90% on a certain test, this means that the test
has failed to show the individual differences among those students probably because the questions were very easy. Similarly, if all students
score between 20% and 30%, this test has failed again to discriminate students probably because all questions were very difficult.

6. Time. Sometimes a test a fails to be a good one because it gives much less or much more time than necessary. Inadequate or overadequate durations usually result in very low or very high scores respectively, which
is undesirable in both cases.

However, from these six characteristics there are two that need spe- cial consideration and more illustration. These two are validity and reliability, which will be discussed in detail in the coming sections.

VII. 7. 1. Validity :

Validity is one of the major qualities of a good test and it may be clas- sified into three main types :

1. Face validity. Face validity implies that a general look at a certain test

115

should be enough to decide whether the test is valid or not. For example, if a test aims at the evaluation of spelling only and at the same includes questions on punctuation, it is obvious that such a test lacks face validity.

2. Curricular validity. Curricular validity is sometimes called content validity. Such validity is obtained through making the test as repre- sentative of the subject matter as possible. Of course, the test cannot include all the subject matter. It only selects a sample that should be large enough and varied enough to represent the whole material satisfactorily.

3. Concurrent validity. Concurrent validity is a statistical one, where students' scores on a certain test are compared to their scores on another test wider in area than the first one. For example, a test on voca- bulary may be compared to a comprehensive test on language with all its aspects. The scores of both tests are then processed into certain satisti- cal formulas to obtain validity co-efficient, which is to be determined if it is significant or not.

In fact, it may be difficult for most teachers to work on the last type of validity, i.e., concurrent validity, because this requires sufficient knowledge of statistics. However, the teacher can and should secure both face validity and content validity for his tests so as to make tests purposeful and representative. Face validity implies continuous sticking to the purpose of the test and thus connecting each item to that purpose. Content validity implies comprehensionveness : the test is a representative sample of the tested subject.

VII. 7. 2. Reliability :

Reliability is another major quality of a good test. It may be classified into three basic types :

1. Scoring reliability.   Scoring reliability means that marking the same answers is consistent when they are re-marked by the same persons or other persons. To put it differently, scoring reliability implies objectivity of marking students' answers. Such reliability is to be statistically computed and its co-efficient is to be checked for significance.

2. Temporal reliability. To check temporal reliability, the same test is taken again by the same students after a certain period of time long enough to let students forget how they respond to each item in the first

test but short enough to minimize probable additional learning. Besides, the second test may be identical with the first one or parallel to it in con- tent and difficulty. Then scores on both tests are compared and reliability co-efficient is computed.

This type of reliability is also called test-retest reliability because the same test or a parallel one is repeated. As result, what is excepted is that scores on both tests should be generally close. If not so, this indi- cates there is something wrong with the tests such as cheating, blind guessing, vague questions, or unclear instructions.

3. Internal reliability or split-half reliability. Internal reliability is computed by splitting the test into two halves: items of odd numbers and items of even numbers. Each student gets two scores for his answer sheet with a score for each half. The correlation between the two sets of scores is calculated and the co-efficient is judged to be significant or not.

The expected outcome is that the should be a high positive corre- lation between the scores on the two halves. Otherwise, this will be an indication that there is something unusual with the test, which needs to be modified or expanded.

Nevertheless, it must be admitted that the average teacher may not be able to work on these reliability types because they require some so- phisticated knowledge of statistics. However, the teacher can do several things in order to increase the reliability of his tests:

1. Instructions on how the student should answer have to be clear, because ambiguous instructions usually weaken reliability.

2. The luck factor in obtaining scores should be eliminated or at least minimized by controlling the nature of questions and increasing the number of choices when recognition is involved.

3. The test has to be reasonably long. Holding other variables cons- tant, a long test is more reliable than a short one.

4. Cheating is to be absolutely forbidden and strictly dealt with.

5. Blind guessing is to be eliminated or kept to the minimum because it damages consistency of test scores. To stop such guessing, a penalty for wrong answers may be used and a correction of statements recognized to be wrong may be required.

VII. 8. Discussion :

1. What are the purposes of foreign language testing ?

2. Make a ten-item test on any language skill you choose. Then determine what type of test it is in light of the classification of tests given in this chapter.

3. Make a comprehensive written examination of two hours to eva- luate students' English in any secondary year you choose. Test grammar, vocabulary, spelling, pronunciation, and punctuation and make your ques- tions as varied as varied as possible.

4. What are the advantages and disadvantages of each the follow-ing : true-false questions, multiple choice, and matching tests?

5. What is your opinion of penalty for wrong answers in multiple choice tests ?

6. For each language skill, determine which test forms are for pro- duction and which ones for recognition.

7. Take an already prepared test on English. Evaluate it as to form, content, validity, scorability, and design.

8. Concerning the different tests on language skills, which tests evaluate one single ability and which ones evaluate a combination of abili- ties ? Explain how.

TEACHING AIDS

The teacher is urged to benefit, as much as he can, from aids in teaching foreign languages. These aids are of various types. Firstly, there are aids that are solely visual, e.g., the chalkboard, pictures, charts, and flash cards. Secondly, there are aids are solely aural, e.g., radio and tapes. Thirdly, there are aids that simultaneously visual and aural, e.g., motion pictures and television. In the following sections, we shall see how and when each aid may be used and acquainted with the limitations of each aid.

VIII. 1. Chalkboard :

The chalkboard can offer the greatest help to the teacher. It may be used for different purposes such as :

1. The teacher writes the date, lesson, part, and page on the chalk- board at the. beginning of his period.

2. The chalkboard is used to write new vocabulary items and their meanings.

3. It is also used in the presentation of new grammatical structures.

4. It is used to write questions to be answered by students in the cases of practice and testing.

5. The teacher uses the chalkboard to write assignments for home- work.

7. He uses the chalkboard to demonstrate model handwriting.

8. He uses it to draw some pictures or diagrams to explain some dif- faculties.

9. He may ask students to write words or sentences on the chalk- board to check the correctness of spelling or structure.

10. He may use it to write model answers for a test or an exercise followed by collective correction of mistakes.

As a matter of fact, those are just examples of the different usages of the chalkboard. In addition, one can easily notice that the chalkboard has several advantages over some other aids :

1. The chalkboard exists in every classroom. Actually, it is consi- dered an essential part of the classroom.

2. It is a simple aid devoid of any technical complexity. Therefore, it can be easily used without any special any training.

3. It is effective for a wide variety of purposes and functions.

4. It is relatively cheap if compared to some other aids. The only co- equipment needed is an eraser and chalk.

5.   Finally, it is cheaply and easily maintained.

However, this does not mean that chalkboard is to be used hap- hazardly or thoughtlessly. It must be used with attention to the following:

1. The teacher has to use the chalkboard neatly through dividing it into three columns or more to maximize benefiting from the space avail- able.

2. The teacher has to use the chalkboard in an orderly manner with- out jumping from one side to anther. Each column has to be filled before moving to the next.

3. The teacher should use colored chalkboard purposefully and not for mere decoration. Besides, over-usage of colored chalk is self-defeating because it causes the loss of its effect.

4. The teacher has to write on the chalkboard so heavily that every student in the classroom can see easily.

5. Not only that, the letters themselves have to be large and clear enough to be easily perceived by all students.

VIII. 2. Pictures :

Pictures are another visual aid and may be used for the following pur- poses :

1. Pictures are good at achieving what may be called the collective eye of the class : students are made to focus their attention on one thing
at the same time. In this respect, pictures and the chalkboard are similar
in function.

2. Pictures may be used in teaching the meanings of new words through word-picture association.
3. Pictures may be used as stimuli to conversation and other similar oral activities.

4. Pictures may supply situations suitable for practicing some gram- matical structures that are taught for the first time or reviewed.

5. Pictures may function as visual cues in substitution drills.

6. A picture may be used a topic of a written composition on descriptive or narrative themes.

7. A picture may be used as an aid in explaining the content of some reading material.

8. Pictures can introduce some sort of variety and, consequently, be
a source of external motivation in the foreign language lesson.

However, one has to remember these points before and while using pictures :

1. Pictures are not always photographed or printed. They may be drawn by teachers or students. In fact, some students are quite skillful at drawing and do wait for an opportunity to exhibit their skills.

2. Pictures prove more effective in teaching present tenses than in teaching past or future ones owing to the present-time suggestions impli-
cit in pictures by their very nature.

3. The picture need not be too detailed.

4. A picture of a certain being should not be usually used when the being itself is available. For example, there is no point in drawing the pic- tures of pens, pencils, and desks when there are dozens of these articles existent in their concrete form in the classroom.

VIII. 3. Flash Cards :

Flash cards are another visual aid mainly used to teach reading. These cards may be of different colors and sizes with words, phrases, or sen- tences written in one side or both sides of each card. The card is shown
to the class for a few seconds and then students are required to say what they have just seen. These cards are helpful in several ways :

1. Flash cards train students to widen their eye span by urging them
to catch large reading units a glance. The urge comes from students' exposure to fairly long units under the pressure of time.

2. These cards help students increase their reading speed because
they become gradually accustomed to perceiving several words as a total- izes whole.

3. Flash cards bring to the classroom atmosphere some kind of desi- rable competition, which normally speeds up students' performance rate
of reading, a phenomenon verified by experimentation.

4. Flash cards bring to the class some change, variation , and refresh- ing feelings, all of which are additional sources of motivation, which is ne- cessary for attention, which is essential for learning.

VIII. 4. Charts :

Charts are cards of reasonable sizes and may be with or without illus- trative pictures. These charts may contain the letters of the alphabet,
selected words, special sentences, idioms, proverbs , the months of the
year, the days of the week, or any other learning material the teacher
wants to reinforce in students' memories. Such reinforcement is attained through fixing those charts o the classroom walls for a duration of time ranging between a week and the whole year.

These wall charts are not useful as a reinforcement means only, but
they are equally useful in several other ways as well:

1. The teacher may use the material on the charts for occasional cho- ral or individual reading.

2. The words written on wall charts are suitable as cues in substitu- tion drills. The teacher points at the word on a certain chart and the stu- dent responds by placing the cue word in the key sentence.

3. These charts function as sources of permanent reinforcement of previously taught material because they remain under students perception
for a long duration of time.

4. The very process of making charts is an activity that involves an opportunity for self-realization, by which students themselves writes and
draw on charts under the teacher's supervision.

5. Charts made by students are one application of the theory of learning by doing.

6. Charts may be also used as a means to encourage students to improve their handwriting. The teacher may ask each student in his class
to prepare a chart and tell them in advance he will stick to the class-
room wall the neatest charts only. This competition usually motivates
children to do their best.

Finally, one has to remember that a good chart should meet some requirements. a good chart must be large enough to be seen by all stu- dents in the classroom. further, it must be clear enough to be legible and neat enough to be attractive.

VIII. 5. Tapes :

Tapes are an aural aid that may be employed for more than one purpose:

1. Tapes may be used to provide students with recorded samples of native speakers' pronunciation and intonation. Students are exposed to
these recordings repeatedly so as to catch the different aspects of pro nuciation such as stresses, pitches, terminals, and phonemes. These
tapes may be a part of a language laboratory or a part of a tap recorder brought to the classroom. Students may just listen to the recorded material or repeat after each utterance depending on the design followed dur-
ing recording.

2. Tapes may be used in grammar drills. Students listen to a recorded sentence, at the end of which there is a pause long enough for students to repeat that sentence or answer if   the sentence is an interrogation.
In addition, the tape may give a cue and then a student gives a response followed by the correct response on the tape, which is finally followed by a choral repetition of the whole class.

3. Tapes may be used in aural comprehension. Students listen to a

story or a passage recorded on a tape. Then they are given written or oral questions to answer.

However, it must be pointed out here that tape recordings have no magic in teaching a foreign language. If students listen to tapes for a short time, the teaching outcome is most probably very limited. On the other hand, if they over-listen to tapes, this will most probably be at the expense of other language skills such as reading and writing. In fact, a great deal depends on the foreign language program, its goals, and duration.

In addition, when tapes are used, the teacher is reminded to consider the following:

1. Tapes are not to be overused in order not to sacrifice other lan- guage skills.

2. Tapes are not the best medium of learning for some students. As a matter of fact, research has shown that average students prefer learning through the eye to learning through the ear.

3. The recording on the tape has to be technically and sonically clear. Experience has shown that ill-recorded tapes are utterly useless and a mere waste of time. Not only that, but such tapes may be almost a real torture to teachers and students alike.

4. The speed of recorded speech has to suit the learners' level. It often happens that a native speaker records some material on tapes so quickly that students cannot understand what they hear and consequently, cannot repeat or respond. Actually, the speed of speech comprehensible to native speakers of a certain language is higher than the speed compre- hensible to foreign speakers of that language.

5. If sentences are recorded to be repeated, they must be short enough to be grasped and then reiterated by students. If the sentence is a long one, it should be broken into shorter units when recorded. Otherwise, the tape has to be continually played back and forward to help students catch a long sentence, which will be an impractical, tedious, and boring task.

6. If recording is designed for intervening repetition or response by students, the pause between each recorded unit and the following one must be adequate for a specific group of students to respond. If the pause is inadequate, conducting such a drill will be quite troublesome.

VIII. 6. Other Aids :

In addition to the previously mentioned aides, there are other ones probably more expensive and, therefore, used at a narrow scale such as:

1. Slides. Slides are pictured projected on a screen by a slide pro- jector.

2. Films strips. They are slides in one film roll.

3. Opaque projector. This opaque projector is an apparatus that can project any picture or written on a screen in a darkened room.

4. Overhead projector. This projector reflects whatever the teacher writes on a special film in front of him.

5. Motion pictures. They may be the most effective aid because they consist of picture, color, sound, and movement combined together in a realistic and interesting manner.

6. Television. Television may offer programs that help teachers and students. Such programs supplement the teacher but cannot take his place. Though television has its own limitations, it introduces change, mo- tivation, entertainment, and additional learning opportunities into the class- room situation.

VIII. 7. Discussion :

1. What aids can students make with their teachers' guidance ?

2. What are the qualities of each of the following : good tapes, good pictures, good flash cards, good charts, effective usage of the chalkboard ?

ABBREVIATIONS

This book includes the following abbreviations:

E = English

EFL = English as a foreign language

F = foreign

L = language

N = native

NL = native language

T = teaching

TEFL = teaching English as a foreign language

FLT = foreign language teaching

SELECTED BIBLIOGRAPHY

Abercromble, David. *Problems and Principles in Language Study*. London: Longmans, Green and Co. Ltd. 1998.

Akin, Johnnye, et al (compliers). *Language Behavior*. The Hague, the Netherlands: Mouton and Co.N.V., 1990.

Allen, Harold B., ed. *Teaching English as a Second Language*. New York: McGraw-Hill Book Company, 1995.

_____, ed, *Readings in Applied English Linguistics*: Second ed. New York: Appleton-Century-Crofts, 1994.

Anderson, John M. *The Grammar of Case*. Cambridge: Cambridge University Press, 1991.

Atherton, John. *Guidance and Practice in English*. London: Hulton Educational Publications, 1992.

Bach, Emmon. *An introduction of Transformational Grammars*. New York: Holt, Rinehart, and Winston, 1994.

_____ and Harms, Robert T., ed. *Universals in Linguistic Theory*. London: Holt, Rinehart, and Wiston, 1998.

Bailey, Dudley, ed. *Introductory Language Essays*. New York: Norton and Company, Inc., 1995.

Bailey, Matilda et al. *Our English Language*. New York: American Book Company, 1996.

Ball, W.J. Conversational English. London: Longmans, Green and Co. Ltd., 1992.

Best, John W. *Research in Education*. New Delhi: Prentice-Hall of India,1993.

Black, Max. *Language and Philosophy*. New York: Cornell University Press, 1990.

127

_____,ed. *The Imortance of Language*. Englewood Cliffs, N.J.: Prentice-Hall, Inc., 1992.

Bourne, Lyle E. *Human Conceptual Behavior*. Boston: Allyn and Bacon, Inc., 1996.

Breal, Michel. *Semantics*. Translated by H. Cust. New York: Dover Publications, Inc., 1994.

Brooks, Nelson. *Language and Language Learning*. Second ed. New York: Harcourt, Brace and World, Inc., 1994.

Brubacher, John S. a history of the Problems of Education. New York: Mc-Graw-Hill Book Company, Inc., 1997.

Bumpass, Faye L. *Teaching Young Students English as a Foreign Language*. New York: American Book Company, 1993.

Carroll, John B. *The Study of Language*. Cambridge, Massachusetts: Harvard University Press, 1996.

Cecco, John P. *The Psychology of Language, Thought, and Instruction*: New York: Holt, Rinehart and Winston, 1999.
_____. *The Psychology of Learning and Instruction*. Englewood Clifts, N.J.: Prentice-Hall, Inc., 1998.

Chafe, Wallace L. *Meaning and the Structure of Language*. Chicago: The University of Chicago Press, 1990.

Chomsky, Noam. *Aspects of the theory of Syntax*. Cambridge, Massachusetts: the M.I.T. Press, 1995.
_____. *Syntactic Structures*. The Hague: Mouton and Co., 1997.

_____. *Language and Mind*. Enlarged ed. New York: Harcourt, Brace, Jovanovich, Inc., 1992.

Christophersen, Paul, and Sandved, Arthur O. *An Advanced English Gram-mar* England: Macmillan and Co, Ltd., 1999.

Clark, Donald H., ed. *The Psychology of Education*. New York: The Free Press, 1997.

Clark, Leonard H. and Starr, L.S. *Secondary School Teaching Methods*. Second ed. New York: the Macmillan Company, 1997.

Close, R.A. *English as a Foreign Language*. London: George Allen and Unwin, 1998.

____. *The New English Grammar*. London: George Allen and Unwin,Ltd., 1994.

Colin, David A. *A. Modern Approach to Teaching English*. New York: Van Nostrand, Reinhold Company, 1998.

Cook, Albert B. *Introduction to the English Language*. New York: The Ronald Press Company, 1999.

Cook, Walter A. *Introduction to Tagmemic Analysis*. New York: Holt, Rinehart and Winston, 1999.

Coombs, Clyde H. *A Theory of Data*. Second ed. New York: John Wiley and Sons, Inc., 1997.

Crow, Lester D., and Crow, Alice. *Educational Psychology*. Resvised ed. New York: American Book Co., 1993.

Cutts, Norma E., and Moseley, Nicholas. *Teaching the Bright and Gifted*. Englewood Cliffs, N.J.: Prentice-Hall., Inc., 1997.

Dacanay, F.R. *Techniques and Procedures in Second Language Teaching*. New York: Oceana Publications, 1997.

Dakin, Julian, et al. language in Education. London: Oxford University Press, 1998.

D'Arcais, G.G Flores and Levelt, W.J.M., ed. *Advances in Psycholinguistics*. Nort-Holland Publishing Company, 1990.

Davies, Alan, ed. *Language Testing Symposium*. Second ed. London: Oxford University Press, 1990.

Deese, James, and Hulse, Stewart H. *The Psychology of Learning*. Third ed. New York: McGraw-Hill, Inc., 1997.

Dowine, N.M., and Heath, R.W. *Basic Statistical Methods*. New York: Harper and Row, Publishers, 1999.

Eble, Robert L. *Measuring Educational Achievement*. Englewood Cliffs, N.J.: Prentice-Hall, Inc., 1995.

Eckersley, C.E., and Eckersley, J.M. *A Comprehensive English Grammar*. London: Longmans, Green and Co. Ltd., 1990.

Erimsson, Margurite, et al. *Foreign Languages in the Elementary School*. Englewood Cliffs, N.J.: Prentice-Hall, Inc., 1994.

Finocchairo, Mary. *Teaching Children Foreign Languages*. New York: Mc-Graw-Hill Book Company, 1994.

Firth, J.R. *The Tongues of Man and Speech*. London: Oxford University Press, 1994.

Fishman, Joshuo A. sociolinguistics. Rowley, Meassachusetts: Newbury Houses Publishers, 1991.

Forgus, Ronald H. *Perception*. New York: Mc-Graw-Hill Book Company, 1996.

Francis, W.Nelson. *The English Language*. London: The English Universities Press Ltd., 1997.

Fried, V., ed. *The Prague School of Linguistics and Language Teaching*. London: Oxford University Press, 1992.

Fries, Charles C. *The Structure of English*. London: Longmans, Green and Co. Ltd., 1997.

Gardiner, Alan. *The Theory of Speech and Language*. Second ed. Oxford: The Clarendon Press, 1991.

Gleason, H.A. *An Introduction to Descriptive Linguistics*. Revised ed. New York: Holt, Rinehart and Winston Inc., 1995.

_____, Jr. *Linguistics and English Grammar*. New York: Holt, Rinehart and Winston, Inc., 1995.

Goldstein, Mariam B. *The Teaching of Language in Our Schools*. New York: The Macmillan Company, 1996.

Graff, Willem L. *Language and Languages*. New York: Russell, Inc., 1994.

Greenbaum, S., and Quirk. R. *Elicitation Experiments in English Linguistic Studies in Use and Attitude.* London: Longman Group Ltd., 1990.

Grive, D.W. *English Language Examing.* logos: African University Press, 1994.

Guthrie, E.R. *The Psychology of Learning.* New York: Harper and Brothers Publishers, 1995.

Hansen, Kenneth H. *High School Teaching.* Englewood Cliffs, N.J.: Prentice-Hall, Inc., 1997.

Harding, David H. *The New Pattern of Language Teaching.* London: Longmans, Green and Co. Ltd., 1997

Harris, Irving D. *Emotional Blocks to Learning.* New York: The Free Press of Glencoe, 1991.

Harris, Zellis S. *Structural Linguistics.* Chicago: The University of Chicago Press, 1991.

Harrocks, John E,a:,d Schoonover, Thelma I. *Measurement for Teachers.* Columbus, Ohio: Charles E.Merrill Publishing Company, 1998.

Hawkins, W..F. and Mackin, R. *English Studies Series.* Book I, II, and III. London: Oxford University Press, 1996.

Healey, F.G.. *Foreign Language Teaching in the Universities.* Manchester: Manchester University Press, 1997.

Herdon, Jeanne H. *A Survey of Modern Grammars.* New York: Holt, Rinehart and Winston, Inc., 1990.

Hilgard, Barnest R. *Theories of Learning.* New York: Appleton-Century-Crofts, Inc., 1996.

Hill, Archibald A. *Introduction to Linguistic Structures.* New York: Harcourt, Brace and World, Inc., 1998.

Hill, L.A. *Selected Articles on the Teaching of English as a Foreign Lan-guage.* London: Oxford University Press, 1997.

Hill, Wingred F. *Learning.* Scranton, Pennsylvania: Chandler Publishing Company, 1993.

Hockett, Charles F. *A Course in Modern Linguistics*. New York: The Macmillan Company, 1998.

Hornby, A.S. *A Guide to Patterns and Usage in English*. London: Oxford University Press, 1998.

_____. *The Teaching of Structural Words and Sentence Patterns*. London: Oxford University Press, 1992.

Howatt, Anthony P. R. *programmed Learning and the Language Teacher*. London: Longmans, Green and Co. Ltd., 1999.

Hudson, R.A. *English Complex Sentences*. Amsterdam: North-Holland Publishing Company, 1991.

Huges, John P. *The Science of Language*. New York: Random House,1994.

Hunter, Madeline. *Retention Theory for Teachers*. El Segundo, California: TIP Publications, 1997.

Hutchins, W.J. *The Generation of Syntactic Structures from a Sentence Base*. Amsterdam: North-Holland-Publishing Company, 1991.

Huxley, Renira, and Ingram, Elizabeth, ed. *Language Acquisition: Model and Methods*. London: Academic Press, 1991.

Jacobs, R.A., and Ronsenbaum, P.S. *English Transformational Grammar*. Waltham: Blaisdell Publishing Company, 1998.

Jakobovites, Leon A. *Foreign Language Learning*. Rowley, Massachusetts: Newbury House Publishers, 1990.

Jalling, Hans, ed. *Modern Language Teaching* . London: Oxford University Press, 1998.

Jersild, Arthur T. *Child Psychology*. Sixth ed. Englewood Clifts, N.J.: Prentice Hall, Inc., 1998.

Jespersen, Otto. *Analytic Syntax*. New York: Holt, Rinehart and Winston, Inc., 1999.

Joos, Martin. *The English Verb*. Madison: the University of Wisconsin Press, 1998.

Jordan, A.M. *Measurement in Education*. New York: McGraw-Hill Book Company, 1998.

Kadler, Eric H. *Linguistics and Teaching Foreign Languages*. New York: Van Nostrand Reinhold Company, 1990.

Kehoe, Monika, ed. *Applied Linguistics*. New York: the Macmillan Company, 1998.

Kelly, L.G. *Centuries of Language Teaching*. Rowley, Massachusetts: Newbury House Publishers, 1999.

Kierzek John M., and Gibson, W. *The Macmillan Handbook of English*. Fourth ed. New York: the Macmillan Book Company,1990.

Lado Robert, *Language Testing*. New York: McGraw-Hill Book Company, 1991.

_____. *Language Teaching*. New York: McGraw-Hill, Inc., 1994.

_____, and Fries, Charles. *English Sentence Patterns*. Michigan: the University Of Michigan Press, 1997.

Langacker, Ronald W. *Language and its Structure*. New York: Harcourt, Brace and World, Inc., 1997.

Langedoen, D. Terence. *Essentials of English Grammar*. New York: Holt, Rinehart and Winston, Inc., 1990.

Lee, Gordon C. *Education in Modern America*. New York: Henry Holt and Company, 1993.

Lee, W.R. *Language-Teaching: Games and Contests*. London:Osford University Press, 1995.

Lefevre, Carl A. *Linguistics and the Teaching of Reading*. New York: Mc-Graw-Hill Book Company, 1992.

Lenneberg, Eric H. *Biological Foundations of Language*. New York: John Willey and Sons, Inc., 1997.

Liebert, B. *Linguistics and the New English Teacher*. New York: the Macmillan Co., 1991.

Liles, B.L. *An Introductory Transformational Grammar*. Englewood Clifts, N.J.: Prentice-Hall, Inc., 1991.

Lindquist, E.F., ed. *Educational Measurement*. Menasha, Wisconsin: George Banta Publishing Co., 1996.

Lucio, William H., and McNeil, J.D. *Supervision*: A Synthesis of Thought and Action. New York: McGraw-Hill Book Company, Inc., 1992.

Ludtke, Roy P., and Furness, Edna L. *New Dimensions in the Teaching of English*. Boulder, Colorado: Pruett Press, Inc., 1997.

Lyman, Howard B. *Test Scores and What they Mean*. Englewood Cliffs, N.J.: Prentice-Hall Inc., 1993.

Lyons, John. *Introduction to Theoretical Linguistics*. Cambridge: the University Press, 1998.

Mackey, William Francis. *Language Teaching Analysis*. London: Longmans, Green and Co., Ltd., 1995.

McBurney, James H., and Wrage, E.J. *Guide to Good Speech*. Englewood Cliffs, N.J.: Prentice-Hall, Inc., 1990.

Mcintosh, Angus, and Halliday, M.A.K. *Patterns of Language*. London: Longmans, Green and Co. Ltd., 1996.

McNerney, Chester T. *Educational Supervision*. First ed. New York: Mc-Graw-Hill Book Company, Inc., 1991.

Michael, Ian. *English Grammatical Categories*. Cambridge: University Press, 1990.

Miller, George A. *Language and Communication*. New York: Mc-Graw-Hill Book Company, Inc., 1991.

Morsey, Royal J. *Improving English Instruction*. Boston: Allyn and Bacon, Inc., 1999.

Nasr, Raja T. *The Teaching of English to Arab Students*. London: Longmans, Green and Co. Ltd., 1993.

_____, and Paine, M.J. *The Structural Patterns of English*. London: Longmans Group Ltd., 1992.

Neagley, Ross L., and Evans, N. Dean. *Handbook for Effective Curriculum Development*. Englewood Clifts, N.J.: Prentice-Hall, Inc., 1997.

Nesfield, J.C. *Errors in English Composition*. London: Macmillan and Co. Ot., 1998.

Oldfield, R.C., and Marshall, J.C., ed. *Language*. Harmondsworth, England: Penguin Book Ltd., 1998.

Oliva, Peter F. *The Teaching of Foreign Languages*. Englewood Clifts, N.J: Prentice-Hall, Inc., 1999.

Onions, C.T. *Modern English Syntax*. London: Routledge and Kegan Paul,1991.

Osgood, Charles E., and Sebeok, T.A. ed. *Psycholinguistics*. Bloomington: Indian University Press, 1995.

Otter, H.S. *A Functional Language Examination*. London: Oxford University Press, 1998.

Palmer, Harold E. *The Scientific Study and Teaching of Languages*. London: Oxford University Press, 1998.

_____. *The Principles of Language Study*. London: Oxford University Press, 1994.

_____, and Blandford, F.G *A Grammar of Spoken English* . third ed. Cambridge: A. Heffer and Sons Ltd., 1999.

_____, and Palmer, S. *English Through Actions*. London: Longman Ltd., 1999.

Pietro, R.J. *Language Structures in Contrast*. Rowley, Massachusetts: Newbury House Publishers, 1991.

Pollock, Thomas Clak, et al. *The Macmillan English Series*. New York: the Macmillan Company, 1997.

_____, et al. *Our English Language*. New York: the Macmillan Company, 1995.

_____,et al. essentials of Modern English. New York: the Macmillan Company, 1995.

Potter, Simeon. *Modern Linguistics*. London: Andre Deutesch Limited, 1997.

Pounds, Ralph L., and Garretson, R.L. *Principle of Modern Education*. New York: the Macmillan Company , 1992.

Quirk, Randolph, and Smith, A.H., ed. *The Teaching of English*. London: Oxford University Press, 1999.

Reed, Carroll E., ed. *The Learning of Language*. New York: Applecton-Cen-tury-Crofts, 1991.

Reibel, David A., and Schane, S.A., ed. *Modern Studies in English*. Engle-wood Cliffs, N.J.: Prentice-Hall, Inc., 1999.

Rivers, W.M. *The Psychologist and the Foreign Language Teacher*. Chicago: University of Chicago Press, 1994.

Roberts, Paul. *Patterns of English* .New York: Harcourt, Brace and world, Inc., 1996.

_____. *Understanding English*. New York: Harper and Row, Publishers, 1998.

_____. *English Syntax*. New York: Harcourt, Brace and World,Inc., 1994.

Robins, R.H. *General Linguistics: an Introductory Survey*. London: Lomgman Group Limited, 1991.

Saporta, Sol, ed. *Psycholinguistics*. New York: Holt, Rinehart and Winston, Inc., 1996.

Sheerer, Constance, ed. *Cognition*. New York: Harper and Row, Publishers, 1994.

Searle, Hohn R. *Speech Acts*. Cambridge: the University Press, 1999.

Skinner, C.E. *Educational Psychology*. Fourth ed. Englewood Cilffs, N.J.: Prentice-Hall, Inc., 1999.

Sled, James. *A Short Introduction to English Grammar*. Chicago: Scott, Foresman and Company, 1999.

Smith, Henry P. *Psychology in Teaching*. Second ed. Englewood Clifts, N.J.: Prentice-Hall, Inc., 1992.

Sorenson, Herbert. *Psychology in Education*. Fourth ed. New York: McGraw-Hill Book Company, Inc., 1994.

Spencer, D.H. *Guided Composition Exercises*. London: Longman Group Limited, 1997.

Stack, Edward M. *The Language Laboratory and Modern Language Teaching.* Revised ed. New York: Oxford University Press, 1996.

Stephens, J.M. *Educational Psychology.* Revised ed. New York: Holt, Rinehart and Winston, 1996.

Stern, H.H. *Languages and the Young School Child.* London: Oxford University Press, 1999.

Sturtevant, Edgar H. *An Introduction to Linguistic Science.* New Haven: Yale University Press, 1997.

Tapp, Jack T., ed. *Reinforcement and Behavior.* New York: Academic Press, 1999.

Thomas, Owen. *Transformational Grammar and the Teacher of English.* New York: Holt, Rinehart, and Winston, Inc., 1995.

Thompson, Denys, ed. *Directions in the Teaching of English.* Cambridge: University Press, 1999.

Travers, Robert M.W. *Essentials of Learning.* New York: the Macmillan Company, 1993.

Valette, Rebecca M. *Modern Language Testing.* New York: Harcourt, Brace and World, Inc., 1997.

Walker, Helen M. *Elementary Statistical Methods.* Third ed. New York: Holt Rinehart and Winston, Inc., 1999.

Wallwork. J.F. *Language and Linguistics,* London: Heinemann Educational Books, 1999.

Wilson, Graham, ed. *A Linguistics Reader.* New York: Harper and Row, Publishers, 1997.

Woodworth, R.S., and Marquis, D.G. *Psychology.* Strand: Methuen and Co. Ltd., 1993.

Zandvoort, R.W. *A Handbook of English Grammar.* London: Longmans, Green and Co. Ltd., 1997.

Index

phonetics, 10

phonics method, 72

phonological difference, 31

pictured cue, 50

pictures, 121

pitches, 29

placement, 102

planning a reading lesson, 79,81

plural morpheme, 34, 46

plus juncture, 28

possessive morpheme, 46

post-reading, 79

post-test, 101

prefix, 65

pre-handwriting, 85

pre-reading, 79-82

pre-test, 101

pre-writing, 85

preparation for writing, 98

prepositional, 27

presentation, 58

presentation of meaning, 64

present morpheme, 35,46

primary stress, 25

problem phoneme, 67

production, 33

prognosis, 101

progressive morpheme, 46

progressive substitution, 51

promotion, 101

pronominalization, 55

pronunciation tests, 105-106

props, 33

public tests, 103

punctuation tests, 111-112

purposes of testing, 100-102

persuasive writing, 92

qualitative restrictions, 98

quantitative restrictions, 98-110

quality system, 110

reading aloud, 76-78

reading patterns, 73-82

reading problems, 81

reading purposes, 73

reading stages, 79

recitation, 78

recognition, 33

referent, 63

regularity of vocabulary, 68

reliability, 113,115-117

remedy, 102

replacement, 55

representative ness, 115

retroflex, 30

rising juncture, 28

root, 60,65,107

rounded, 24

school program, 18

school tests, 103

storability, 115

scoring reliability, 116

secondary stress, 25

see and say method, 72

segmental phonemes, 22

segmentals, 25

selective correction, 98

self- evaluation, 100-101

The Author's Books

1. *A Dictionary of Islamic Terms: English-Arabic & Arabic-English*
2. *Simplified English Grammar*
3. *A Dictionary of Education: English- Arabic*
4. *A Dictionary of Theoretical Linguistics: English- Arabic*
5. *A Dictionary of Applied Linguistics: English-Arabic*
6. *Teaching English to Arab Students*
7. *A Workbook for English Teaching Practice*
8. *Programmed TEFL Methodology*
9. *The Teacher of English*
10. *Improve Your English*
11. *A Workbook for English*
12. *Advance /your English*
13. *An Introduction to Linguistics*
14. *Comparative Linguistics: English and Arabic*
15. *A Contrastive Transformational Grammar: English-Arabic*
16. *The Light of Islam*
17. *The Need for Islam*
18. *Traditions of Prophet Muhammad /B1*
19. *Traditions of Prophet Muhammad /B2*
20. *The Truth about Jesus Christ*
21. *Islam and Christianity*
22. *Questions and answers about Islam*
23. *Learn Arabic by Yourself*
24. *The Blessing of Islam*
25. *Why have they chosen Islam?*
26. *The Crisis of Western Civilization*
27. *A Comparison between the Four Gospels*
28. *Methods of teaching English at the Elementary Stage*
29. *Methods of Teaching English*
30. *Teaching English as a Foreign Language*
31. *Islamic Faith*
32. *Human Rights in Islam*
33. *Penal Codes in Islam*
34. *The Pillars of Islam*

تطلب جميع كتب الدكتور محمد علي الخولي من

مكتبة دار الفلاح - ص. ب ٨١٨ - صويلح ١١٩١٠- الأردن

هاتف وفاكس ٠٠٩٦٢٦-٥٤١١٥٤٧

Printed in the United States
By Bookmasters